To

Jordan Jung
for your beloved birthday

From

Rachel Zowder
the dearest friend in all the world

In the year of our Lord,
the Risen Messiah 2015
April the tenth

A Jane Austen
Devotional

Compiled *and* written *by*
Steffany Woolsey

A Division of Thomas Nelson Publishers

THOMAS NELSON
Since 1798

NASHVILLE   MEXICO CITY   RIO DE JANEIRO

Created by MacKenzie Howard
Cover design by: Studio Gearbox
Managing Editor: Lisa Stilwell

ISBN-13: 978-1-4003-1953-4

Printed in China

14 15 16 17 DSC 8 7 6 5

www.thomasnelson.com

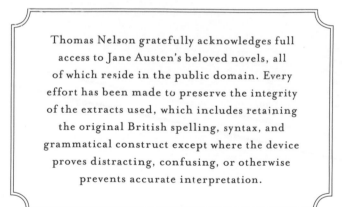

HAVE WE THOUGHT IRREVERENTLY OF THEE,
HAVE WE DISOBEYED THY COMMANDMENTS,
HAVE WE NEGLECTED ANY KNOWN DUTY, OR
WILLINGLY GIVEN PAIN TO ANY HUYMAN
BEING? INCLINE US TO ASK OUR HEARTS THESE
QUESTIONS OH! GOD, AND SAVE US FROM
DECEIVING OURSELVES BY PRIDE AND VANITY.

—*Evening Prayer 1*

TABLE OF CONTENTS

❧

INTRODUCTION

For two centuries now, women have had the opportunity to curl up with a Jane Austen novel and get lost in the romantic stories of the English countryside. It is one of life's great pleasures to finish a book and feel the satisfaction of not only having read a well-crafted story, but of learning a valuable life lesson about God and human nature.

Jane manages to accomplish all of that and more as she shows us through her words what love is. Hers is not a superficial, vain love, but a 1 Corinthians 13 love—one built on action, character, and honor. Any woman who has ever read or seen *Pride and Prejudice* longs for a lover like Mr. Darcy, a hero who comes to her and proclaims, "Surely, you must know it was all for you."

As the ultimate answer to all questions, the Bible is the standard by which we compare everything. Austen's writing is newly illuminated when held up to Scripture. In probing her novels for biblical insights on living and loving, we are reminded of humanity's innate desire for relationship with the Creator. Through Austen's varied and colorful characters, we learn not only about true love but meaningful character. We strive for the humility, wisdom, wit, and grace of a Jane Austen protagonist while learning to recognize the superficial vanity and worldliness of so many other characters who concern themselves only with their own gain.

This book was crafted with the hope that readers would take the opportunity to get lost in the world of Jane Austen—a place where we can all pause in solitude, as though we've just finished a stroll in the garden with Jane and are now sitting down with her to tea, reflecting on important life lessons and taking in the beauty of the countryside. Through excerpts from her work, short devotions, and Scripture, we hope this book will bring you moments of peace while you allow God's Word to shape your own character.

And while you rest for a moment in the simplicity of Jane's words, perhaps your own life will grow a little simpler and more peaceful. Our wish is that through these spiritual insights into Jane's writing, you, too, will grow in the grace and knowledge of our Lord Jesus, who through His death and resurrection woos you with the declaration, "Surely, you must know it was all for you."

Jane did her readers a great service when she used the gift God gave her to touch the world with her writing and wisdom. May each of us do the same with our own talent, and offer glory to God and beauty to our fellow man.

BEING GENEROUS

"Upon my word," said Mr. Dashwood, "I believe you are perfectly right. My father certainly could mean nothing more by his request to me than what you say. I clearly understand it now, and I will strictly fulfill my engagement by such acts of assistance and kindness to them as you have described. When my mother removes into another house my services shall be readily given to accommodate her as far as I can see. Some little present of furniture too may be acceptable then."

"Certainly," returned Mrs. John Dashwood. "But, however, one thing must be considered. When your father and mother moved to Norland, though the furniture of Stanhill was sold, all the china, plate, and linen was saved, and is now left to your mother. Her house will therefore be almost completely fitted up as soon as she takes it."

"That is a material consideration undoubtedly. A valuable legacy indeed! And yet some of the plate would have been a very pleasant addition to our own stock here."

"Yes; and the set of breakfast china is twice as handsome as what belongs to this house. A great deal too handsome, in my opinion, for any place they can ever afford to live in. But, however, so it is. Your father thought only of them. And I must say this: that you owe no particular gratitude to him, nor attention to his wishes; for we very well know that if he could, he would have left almost everything in the world to them."

This argument was irresistible. It gave to his intentions whatever of decision was wanting before; and he finally resolved, that it would be absolutely unnecessary, if not highly indecorous, to do more for the widow and children of his father, than such kind of neighbourly acts as his own wife pointed out.

—Sense and Sensibility

So ends a series of exchanges between Mr. and Mrs. John Dashwood to settle on how much—if anything—to give his father's widow and her three daughters. You can see Mrs. Dashwood's mean-spiritedness at battle with Mr. Dashwood's natural goodwill and generosity.

Sadly, uncharitable living is not limited to small-minded persons like Mrs. Dashwood. It is a matter of the heart: any one of us is prone to greed if we cultivate qualities such as self-interest, pride, and selfishness, for "what comes out of the mouth proceeds from the heart, and *this defiles a person*" (Matthew 15:18, emphasis added). The Dashwoods' self-congratulatory tone in the final section clearly reveals defiled hearts.

In the book of Mark, Jesus teaches His disciples what real generosity looks like: "A poor widow came and put in two small copper coins, which make a penny. And [Jesus] called his disciples to him and said to them, 'Truly, I say to you, this poor widow has put in more than all those who are contributing to the offering box. For they all contributed out of their abundance, but she out of her poverty has put in everything she had, all she had to live on'" (12:42–44).

As Christ followers, we are called to imitate the widow who gave no less than "everything she had." When we choose this route, He can begin to develop in us qualities such as generosity, kindness, and compassion. We live like Christ by serving others and giving freely of our time and resources. We look like Him by doing so joyfully and thankfully.

❧

THE GENEROUS SOUL WILL BE MADE RICH.

Proverbs 11:25 NKJV

3

CHRIST'S UNCONDITIONAL LOVE

"[Our daughters] have none of them much to recommend them," replied [Mr. Bennet]; "they are all silly and ignorant like other girls; but Lizzy has something more of quickness than her sisters."

"Mr. Bennet, how can you abuse your own children in such way? You take delight in vexing me. You have no compassion on my poor nerves."

"You mistake me, my dear. I have a high respect for your nerves. They are my old friends. I have heard you mention them with consideration these twenty years at least."

"Ah! you do not know what I suffer."

"But I hope you will get over it, and live to see many young men of four thousand a year come into the neighbourhood."

"It will be no use to us if twenty such should come, since you will not visit them."

"Depend upon it, my dear, that when there are twenty I will visit them all."

Mr. Bennet was so odd a mixture of quick parts, sarcastic humour, reserve, and caprice, that the experience of three and twenty years had been insufficient to make his wife understand his character. Her mind was less difficult to develope. She was a woman of mean understanding, little information, and uncertain temper. When she was discontented, she fancied herself nervous. The business of her life was to get her daughters married; its solace was visiting and news.

—Pride and Prejudice

Mrs. Bennet's ill breeding is on display from the onset of *Pride and Prejudice*. Noisy and foolish, she lacks even basic manners or social skills. Her single, driving life's focus—finding eligible husbands for her five daughters—is so exhaustive that over the course of the book she will succeed in driving away nearly every potential suitor.

Mrs. Bennet's intellectual shortcomings are in stark contrast to her husband's dry humor and quick wit. Twenty-three years prior, Mr. Bennet chose to marry a silly but pretty wife, and it seems clear that he daily regrets his choice. To compensate for his unhappy marriage, he withdraws into his study and takes pleasure in books, teasing his wife, and indulging his sarcastic humor. His favoritism of smart, funny Lizzy only further elevates his superiority toward his wife and deepens the chasm between them.

Comical though it may be, Mr. Bennet's poorly executed role as patriarch runs counter to the Bible's directive to husbands: "Love your wives, as *Christ loved the church and gave himself up for her.* . . . He who loves his wife loves himself" (Ephesians 5:25, 28, emphasis added).

Jesus didn't wait until we deserved His love to give it to us. Instead, He committed to love us first. This required serious sacrifice—the same kind of sacrifice a husband and wife should commit to each other, even when the other is acting neither lovingly nor attractively.

Christ's example teaches us this: love is not first and foremost about finding our spouses physically, emotionally, or intellectually our equals. It is about the commitment to love . . . *no matter what.*

❦

I WILL BETROTH YOU TO ME IN FAITHFULNESS. AND
YOU SHALL KNOW THE LORD.

Hosea 2:20

Vanity's Folly

Vanity was the beginning and the end of Sir Walter Elliot's character; vanity of person and of situation. He had been remarkably handsome in his youth; and, at fifty-four, was still a very fine man. Few women could think more of their personal appearance than he did, nor could the valet of any new made lord be more delighted with the place he held in society. He considered the blessing of beauty as inferior only to the blessing of a baronetcy; and the Sir Walter Elliot, who united these gifts, was the constant object of his warmest respect and devotion.

His good looks and his rank had one fair claim on his attachment; since to them he must have owed a wife of very superior character to any thing deserved by his own. Lady Elliot had been an excellent woman, sensible and amiable; whose judgement and conduct, if they might be pardoned the youthful infatuation which made her Lady Elliot, had never required indulgence afterwards.—She had humoured, or softened, or concealed his failings, and promoted his real respectability for seventeen years; and though not the very happiest being in the world herself, had found enough in her duties, her friends, and her children, to attach her to life, and make it no matter of indifference to her when she was called on to quit them.—Three girls, the two eldest sixteen and fourteen, was an awful legacy for a mother to bequeath, an awful charge rather, to confide to the authority and guidance of a conceited, silly father.

—Persuasion

For Sir Walter Elliot, vanity has its tentacles wrapped around both his "person" (appearance) and "situation" (title). Even his seventeen-year marriage to the good Lady Elliot, a woman of "very superior character," who humored his arrogance and concealed his failings, was not enough to dethrone his "conceited, silly" ways.

In speaking to the folly of vanity, there is perhaps no greater authority than King Solomon. Born into royalty and appointed to the throne at age twelve, Solomon had a bright future. He was beloved by his subjects and granted unlimited wisdom *and* riches by God! But over the course of a long life, Solomon was not strong enough to withstand the temptations that come with great luxury. He had more than seven hundred wives, and eventually they turned his heart away from the one true God and led him into idolatry.

The book of Ecclesiastes contains many of Solomon's ruminations on the emptiness of a life derailed by vain pleasures: "I have seen all the works that are done under the sun; and indeed, all is vanity and grasping for the wind" (1:14 NKJV). Even the wisest king of Israel lived to regret how he squandered God's blessings.

Solomon's advice can help us avoid the same fate: we will not find the meaning of life in knowledge, money, pleasure, work, or popularity. True satisfaction comes from the pursuit of godly wisdom, appreciating it as His gift, and using what we learn for His glory.

❧

THE BEGINNING OF WISDOM IS THIS: GET WISDOM,
AND WHATEVER YOU GET, GET INSIGHT.

Proverbs 4:7

FAITHFULNESS

Sir Thomas [Bertram] was fully resolved to be the real and consistent patron of [his niece, Fanny Price], and Mrs. Norris had not the least intention of being at any expense whatever in her maintenance. As far as walking, talking, and contriving reached, she was thoroughly benevolent, and nobody knew better how to dictate liberality to others; but her love of money was equal to her love of directing, and she knew quite as well how to save her own as to spend that of her friends.

Having married on a narrower income than she had been used to look forward to, she had, from the first, fancied a very strict line of economy necessary; and what was begun as a matter of prudence, soon grew into a matter of choice, as an object of that needful solicitude which there were no children to supply. Had there been a family to provide for, Mrs. Norris might never have saved her money; but having no care of that kind, there was nothing to impede her frugality, or lessen the comfort of making a yearly addition to an income which they had never lived up to. Under this infatuating principle, counteracted by no real affection for her sister, it was impossible for her to aim at more than the credit of projecting and arranging so expensive a charity; though perhaps she might so little know herself as to walk home to the Parsonage, after this conversation, in the happy belief of being the most liberal-minded sister and aunt in the world.

—*Mansfield Park*

Mrs. Norris has just talked her brother-in-law, Sir Thomas Bertram, into inviting his niece Fanny to live at Mansfield Park. Mrs. Norris has given the impression that she will bear partial responsibility for her niece's upbringing, but in reality, she has no intention of ever doing so and will always have a ready excuse for evading such a burden. She cares only to project the *image* of charity, not actually to follow through with it.

In the parable of the talents, Jesus addresses the importance of blessing others with our talents, not just using them for show: "The man who had received the five talents went at once and put his money to work and gained five more. So also, the one with the two talents gained two more. But the man who had received the one talent went off, dug a hole in the ground and hid his master's money" (Matthew 25:16–18 NIV). Jesus' parable further reveals that the two servants who returned the most were deemed "faithful" by their master, but the one who hid his bag was berated for lack of faithfulness.

Notice the master's focus: faithfulness. This parable isn't instructing believers to increase wealth for the kingdom— our God already owns the cattle on a thousand hills. Rather, it demonstrates the importance of using our time, energy, and resources to bless others. The choice between using what we've been given and hoarding it for ourselves indicates how much we truly love our Master.

❧

"FOR EVERYONE WHO HAS WILL BE GIVEN MORE, AND HE WILL HAVE AN ABUNDANCE. WHOEVER DOES NOT HAVE, EVEN WHAT HE HAS WILL BE TAKEN FROM HIM."

Matthew 25:29 NIV

Unhealthy Friendships

"I do not know what your opinion may be, Mrs. Weston," said Mr. Knightly, "of this great intimacy between Emma and Harriet Smith, but I think it a bad thing."

"A bad thing! Do you really think it a bad thing?—why so?"

"I think they will neither of them do the other any good."

"You surprise me! Emma must do Harriet good: and by supplying her with a new object of interest, Harriet may be said to do Emma good. I have been seeing their intimacy with the greatest pleasure. How very differently we feel!" . . .

"[Emma] will never submit to any thing requiring industry and patience, and a subjection of the fancy to the understanding. Where Miss Taylor failed to stimulate, I may safely affirm that Harriet Smith will do nothing. . . . Emma is spoiled by being the cleverest of her family. At ten years old, she had the misfortune of being able to answer questions which puzzled her sister at seventeen. . . . I think [Harriet Smith] the worst sort of companion that Emma could possibly have. She knows nothing herself, and looks upon Emma as knowing every thing. She is a flatterer in all her ways; and so much the worse, because undersigned. Her ignorance is hourly flattery. How can Emma imagine she has any thing to learn herself, while Harriet is presenting such a delightful inferiority? And as for Harriet, I will venture to say that she cannot gain by the acquaintance. Hartfield will only put her out of conceit with all the other places she belongs to. She will grow just refined enough to be uncomfortable with those among whom birth and circumstance have placed her home. I am much mistaken if Emma's doctrines give any strength of mind, or tend at all to make a girl adapt herself rationally to the varieties of her situation in life.—They only give her a little polish."

—*Emma*

This repartee—which takes place between the insightful Mr. Knightly and Emma's beloved former governess, Mrs. Weston—exposes serious flaws in Harriet and Emma's seemingly innocent friendship.

To be certain, Emma *is* generous with her resources. She is also—as Mrs. Weston rushes to point out—clever, pretty, earnest, kind, and well-intentioned. All are good qualities to possess. But are they enough?

In *Emma*, we see young Miss Woodhouse use her vast resources to "help" the disadvantaged, like Harriet. But through Mr. Knightley's eyes, we recognize that this does not render Emma's motive pure—nor does Harriet's innocent flattery, admiration, and high regard for Emma absolve *her* of blame.

In other words, the two do nothing to build each other's character. Such a shaky premise nearly guarantees calamity! The Bible warns against the company of fools: "A fool hath no delight in understanding, but that his heart may discover itself" (Proverbs 18:2 KJV).

We must choose our friends carefully. Any friendship not centered around Christ, and particularly those built on mutual foolishness, is a pathway to ruin.

Like Mr. Knightley, make a bold assessment of your friendships. Then strive to point one another to Christ, not each other—and see where He leads.

❧

HE WHO WALKS WITH WISE MEN WILL BE WISE,
BUT THE COMPANION OF FOOLS WILL BE DESTROYED.

Proverbs 13:20 NKJV

BUILDING CHARACTER

Some mothers might have encouraged the intimacy from motives of interest, for Edward Ferrars was the eldest son of a man who had died very rich; and some might have repressed it from motives of prudence, for, except a trifling sum, the whole of his fortune depended on the will of his mother. But Mrs. Dashwood was alike uninfluenced by either consideration. It was enough for her that he appeared to be amiable, that he loved her daughter, and that Elinor returned the partiality. It was contrary to every doctrine of hers that difference of fortune should keep any couple asunder who were attracted by resemblance of disposition; and that Elinor's merit should not be acknowledged by every one who knew her, was to her comprehension impossible.

Edward Ferrars was not recommended to their good opinion by any peculiar graces of person or address. He was not handsome, and his manners required intimacy to make them pleasing. He was too diffident to do justice to himself; but when his natural shyness was overcome, his behaviour gave every indication of an open, affectionate heart. His understanding was good, and his education had given it solid improvement. But he was neither fitted by abilities nor disposition to answer the wishes of his mother and sisters, who longed to see him distinguished—as—they hardly knew what. They wanted him to make a fine figure in the world in some manner or other. His mother wished to interest him in political concerns, to get him into parliament, or to see him connected with some of the great men of the day. Mrs. John Dashwood wished it likewise; but in the mean while, till one of these superior blessings could be attained, it would have quieted her ambition to see him driving a barouch. But Edward had no turn for great men or barouches. All his wishes centered in domestic comfort and the quiet of private life.

—Sense and Sensibility

Immediately upon introduction, Edward Ferrars is described as affable, gentle, and amiable. His manners are pleasing, and his affectionate heart is evident to all who encounter him. While Mrs. Dashwood sees and appreciates these qualities in Edward's character, his own mother and sister would prefer that he become . . . *someone*. They long to see him distinguished, to hold a position that commands respect—and preferably one outfitted with a barouche!

This divergent view of Edward is best summarized by Proverbs 16:19: "Better to live humbly with the poor than to share plunder with the proud" (NLT). Yes, Edward is positioned to become a very wealthy man; and certainly his education carries potential for high office. Yet he is clearly unmoved by material considerations. Somehow, his character remains unspoiled.

The difference of opinion between the two mothers boils down to character versus position. While Mrs. Ferrars laments her son's natural shyness, his diffidence, and his lack of ambition, Mrs. Dashwood seems to understand that it is better to be *humble and poor* than *rich and proud*.

Like Edward's mother and sister, do you attach importance to a high position—either for yourself or for others? Or do you admire the qualities that meet with Mrs. Dashwood's approval—Edward's meek and gentle spirit, his contrite heart, and his interests centered in "domestic comfort" and quiet "private life"? Perhaps your answer defines your own character.

❦

BLESSED ARE THE UNDEFILED IN THE WAY,
WHO WALK IN THE LAW OF THE LORD!

Psalm 119:1 NKJV

Judging Others Hastily

Mr. Bingley was good looking and gentlemanlike; he had a pleasant countenance, and easy, unaffected manners. His brother-in-law, Mr. Hurst, merely looked the gentleman; but his friend Mr. Darcy soon drew the attention of the room by his fine, tall person, handsome features, noble mien; and the report which was in general circulation within five minutes after his entrance, of his having ten thousand a year. The gentlemen pronounced him to be a fine figure of a man, the ladies declared he was much handsomer than Mr. Bingley, and he was looked at with great admiration for about half the evening, till his manners gave a disgust which turned the tide of his popularity; for he was discovered to be proud, to be above his company, and above being pleased; and not all his large estate in Derbyshire could then save him from having a most forbidding, disagreeable countenance, and being unworthy to be compared with his friend.

Mr. Bingley had soon made himself acquainted with all the principal people in the room; he was lively and unreserved, danced every dance, was angry that the ball closed so early, and talked of giving one himself at Netherfield. Such amiable qualities must speak for themselves. What a contrast between him and his friend! Mr. Darcy danced only once with Mrs. Hurst and once with Miss Bingley, declined being introduced to any other lady, and spent the rest of the evening in walking about the room, speaking occasionally to one of his own party. His character was decided. He was the proudest, most disagreeable man in the world, and every body hoped that he would never come there again. Amongst the most violent against him was Mrs. Bennet, whose dislike of his general behaviour was sharpened into particular resentment by his having slighted one of her daughters.

—*Pride and Prejudice*

*T*wo wealthy gentlemen enter the picture early in *Pride and Prejudice*: Mr. Bingley, pleasant and friendly; Mr. Darcy, handsome and aloof. Though Darcy is at first spoken of in hushed tones for his handsomeness and wealth, his disdainful attitude toward everyone at the ball becomes evident, and the opinion spreads like wildfire that he is "the proudest, most disagreeable man in the world." How fitting that of all who are repulsed by his behavior, it is Mrs. Bennet who takes the greatest offense—because Darcy slighted one of her daughters.

Darcy's character is quickly stamped with the seal of Pride. This all-too-human tendency to judge others in haste—to form a "prejudice" based not upon fact but on superficial observation—is one of the central themes of the novel. While Mrs. Bennet is clearly guilty of rash judgment, Darcy and even Elizabeth also commit the same offense. The real problem in criticizing and judging others is that it blinds us to our own sin by keeping us focused on others' shortcomings. This ultimately prevents us from right relationship with Christ. We are instructed, "Examine yourselves as to whether you are in the faith. Test yourselves. Do you not know yourselves, that Jesus Christ is in you?" (2 Corinthians 13:5 NKJV).

The next time you find yourself judging another, be quick to first examine your own heart and behavior. Weed out the sin you find there first. Let your example and guide be Jesus, who always demonstrated a pure and humble heart toward others.

❧

PUT ON THE NEW MAN WHICH WAS CREATED ACCORDING TO
GOD, IN TRUE RIGHTEOUSNESS AND HOLINESS.

Ephesians 4:24 NKJV

IMITATING CHRIST FOR OTHERS

The progress of Catherine's unhappiness from the events of the evening was as follows. It appeared first in a general dissatisfaction with everybody about her, while she remained in the rooms, which speedily brought on considerable weariness and a violent desire to go home. This, on arriving in Pulteney Street, took the direction of extraordinary hunger, and when that was appeased, changed into an earnest longing to be in bed; such was the extreme point of her distress; for when there she immediately fell into a sound sleep which lasted nine hours, and from which she awoke perfectly revived, in excellent spirits, with fresh hopes and fresh schemes. . . .

She sat quietly down to her book after breakfast, resolving to remain in the same place and the same employment till the clock struck one; and from habitude very little incommoded by the remarks and ejaculations of Mrs. Allen, whose vacancy of mind and incapacity for thinking were such, that as she never talked a great deal, so she could never be entirely silent; and, therefore, while she sat at her work, if she lost her needle or broke her thread, if she heard a carriage in the street, or saw a speck upon her gown, she must observe it aloud, whether there were anyone at leisure to answer her or not.

—*Northanger Abbey*

Mrs. Allen—young Catherine's wealthy neighbor from Fullerton—is a woman with "vacancy of mind and incapacity for thinking." She is self-absorbed and shallow, thinking only of bonnets and gowns and balls, unable to contribute intellectually to any conversation outside the scope of her limited imagination. It is clear that Mrs. Allen is hardly the role model that young, impressionable Catherine needs at such a critical juncture in her life.

What sort of a mentor makes a proper role model for a young woman like Catherine? In Scripture, we see that in order to set a godly example for other believers, a role model must choose to model her life after the Lord Jesus. Paul, Silas, and Timothy were exemplary of this in 1 Thessalonians 1:5–6: "You paid careful attention to the way we lived among you, and determined to live that way yourselves. In imitating us, you imitated the Master. Although great trouble accompanied the Word, you were able to take great joy from the Holy Spirit!— taking the trouble with the joy, the joy with the trouble" (MSG). These three men looked to and followed Christ's example by actively pursuing disciplines which, over time, developed and deepened their faith and spiritual maturity. Believers in Thessalonica experienced the same by following this lead and, in so doing, imitated Christ themselves.

If you desire to imitate Christ above all else, find a role model whose conduct—words, deeds, choices—reflects a heart untempted by the foolish things of this world. But above all, draw close to the Lord, seek in your own life to be an example to others, and you will grow in wisdom and maturity.

❧

SET THE BELIEVERS AN EXAMPLE IN SPEECH, IN
CONDUCT, IN LOVE, IN FAITH, IN PURITY.

1 Timothy 4:12

THE VIRTUE OF STEADINESS

Harriet was soon back again, and the proposal almost immediately made; and she had no scruples which could stand many minutes against the earnest pressing of both the others. Emma wished to go to work directly, and therefore produced the portfolio containing her various attempts at portraits, for not one of them had ever been finished, that they might decide together on the best size for Harriet. Her many beginnings were displayed. Miniatures, half-lengths, whole-lengths, pencil, crayon, and water-colours had been all tried in turn. She had always wanted to do every thing, and had made more progress both in drawing and music than many might have done with so little labour as she would ever submit to. She played and sang;—and drew in almost every style; but steadiness had always been wanting; and in nothing had she approached the degree of excellence which she would have been glad to command, and ought not to have failed of. She was not much deceived as to her own skill either as an artist or a musician, but she was not unwilling to have others deceived, or sorry to know her reputation for accomplishment often higher than it deserved.

—Emma

A certain virtue is lacking in Emma Woodhouse, and its absence is quite apparent in this charming scene. Emma's failure to ever completely finish a project—be it a water-color painting, a reading list, or an advanced musical composition—is on display here, where she shows Harriet and Mr. Elton her portfolio of half-finished paintings.

Jane Austen describes Emma as lacking the virtue of

steadiness; modern readers might recognize her behavior as lacking in *diligence*. It is, simply put, an inability to stick to something until the job is done.

Perhaps you too struggle with the same issue as Emma. Is it any wonder? In an age of rapid-access information, expanding technology, and sound-bite news clips, we are pulled in a hundred different directions.

This is by no means a criticism of the wonderful advances in communication ushered in by social media and networking. But as with Emma, the danger lies in the ever-present possibility of distraction, in doing every job halfway, in looking for entertainment to rescue us from the task at hand.

It is as important for women today as in Jane Austen's day to develop discipline and steadiness in character. Proverbs 4:23 tells us, "Keep your heart with all diligence, for out of it spring the issues of life" (NKJV). Make no mistake: the choices that govern your time have direct bearing on the way you lead your life.

Do you check e-mail, Facebook, and Twitter daily (perhaps even hourly)? Are more beneficial disciplines—like time in prayer, time with your spouse or children, time spent serving and blessing others—being disrupted or even put on the back burner? Perhaps it is time to examine what activities and interests you let dominate your waking minutes and hours. Pray about how to best spend your time . . . and then choose wisely.

☙

NOW FINISH THE WORK, SO THAT YOUR EAGER
WILLINGNESS TO DO IT MAY BE MATCHED BY YOUR
COMPLETION OF IT, ACCORDING TO YOUR MEANS.

2 Corinthians 8:11 NIV

"Oh [Jane]! you are a great deal too apt, you know, to like people in general. You never see a fault in any body. All the world are good and agreeable in your eyes. I never heard you speak ill of a human being in my life."

"I would wish not to be hasty in censuring any one; but I always speak what I think."

"I know you do; and it is that which makes the wonder. With your good sense, to be honestly blind to the follies and nonsense of others! Affectation of candour is common enough;—one meets it every where. But to be candid without ostentation or design—to take the good of every body's character and make it still better, and say nothing of the bad—belongs to you alone. And so, you like this man's sisters too, do you? Their manners are not equal to his."

"Certainly not; at first. But they are very pleasing women when you converse with them. Miss Bingley is to live with her brother and keep his house; and I am much mistaken if we shall not find a very charming neighbour in her."

Elizabeth listened in silence, but was not convinced. Their behaviour at the assembly had not been calculated to please in general; and with more quickness of observation and less pliancy of temper than her sister, and with a judgment, too, unassailed by any attention to herself, she was very little disposed to approve them.

—*Pride and Prejudice*

lizabeth may be the most intellectual of the Bennet sisters, but Jane is the sweetest: "You never see a fault in any body. All the world are good and agreeable in your eyes. I never heard you speak ill of a human being in my life." In a nutshell, Jane looks for the best in others—and as a result, she invariably finds it.

Throughout *Pride and Prejudice,* Jane's character reflects the golden rule: "Do to others as you would have them do to you" (Luke 6:31 NIV). This verse, spoken by Jesus, is the personal standard He set for dealing with others. Jane lives out this truth by employing a simple philosophy: if we want to be loved, we have to give love. Likewise, if we want meaningful relationships, we need to treat others with respect and esteem. Forgiveness, kindness, generosity—in all these areas, we must lead without expectation of reciprocity.

The benefit of following Jesus' golden rule isn't that we will automatically be rewarded for our efforts, but that we come to see and understand and appreciate the way Christ first loved us. It is almost too much to comprehend when we are living for ourselves; but if we choose to obey Christ's command in doing unto others, we begin to walk in step with Him and His thoughts become our own.

Do you desire a life free from the expectation that you'll always be treated well or get the outcome you think you deserve? Are your thoughts sometimes consumed by life's unfairness? Focus on treating others as Jesus would. Your reward will be a newfound, heartfelt appreciation for how much He loves you.

ᘒᘝᘒ

"SO WHATEVER YOU WISH THAT MEN WOULD DO TO YOU,
DO SO TO THEM; FOR THIS IS THE LAW AND THE PROPHETS."

Matthew 7:12 RSV

HEART'S KINDNESS

A week had passed in this way, and no suspicion of it conveyed by her quiet passive manner, when [Fanny] was found one morning by her cousin Edmund, the youngest of the sons, sitting crying on the attic stairs.

"My dear little cousin," said he, with all the gentleness of an excellent nature, "what can be the matter?" And sitting down by her, he was at great pains to overcome her shame in being so surprised, and persuade her to speak openly. Was she ill? or was anybody angry with her? or had she quarrelled with Maria and Julia? or was she puzzled about anything in her lesson that he could explain? Did she, in short, want anything he could possibly get her, or do for her? For a long while no answer could be obtained beyond a "no, no—not at all—no, thank you"; but he still persevered; and no sooner had he begun to revert to her own home, than her increased sobs explained to him where the grievance lay. He tried to console her.

"You are sorry to leave Mama, my dear little Fanny," said he, "which shows you to be a very good girl; but you must remember that you are with relations and friends, who all love you, and wish to make you happy. Let us walk out in the park, and you shall tell me all about your brothers and sisters."

—Mansfield Park

The kindness Edmund shows Fanny, who has known little kindness in her lifetime, is pure, selfless, and free of motive—this, despite Edmund's being surrounded by selfish, willful, self-important people! It is no wonder that Edmund's good heart and gentle affection for his cousin win Fanny's heart.

In Romans 12:8, we are encouraged to model this sort of kindness: "If your gift is to encourage others, be encouraging! If it is giving, give generously. If God has given you leadership ability, take the responsibility seriously. And if you have a gift for showing kindness to others, do it gladly" (NLT). Showing kindness, as we see in Scripture, is just one way that we get to demonstrate Christ's character to others.

The ultimate example of kindness is Jesus, who reached out to the hurt, the broken, the oppressed, the downtrodden—people like Fanny, who had few friends and fewer resources—and lifted them from their pain and suffering. Then Jesus made the ultimate sacrifice: He stretched out His arms and died for us. None of us ever did anything to deserve this kind of kindness. But that's the beauty of serving our great God: He doesn't treat us as we deserve. He knows our needs and meets us where we are—then empowers us to act like Edmund, by taking steps to meet the needs of others.

❧

HE SAVED US, NOT BECAUSE OF WORKS DONE BY US IN RIGHTEOUSNESS, BUT ACCORDING TO HIS OWN MERCY.

Titus 3:5

ESTEEMING OTHERS

Edward had been staying several weeks in the house before he engaged much of Mrs. Dashwood's attention; for she was, at that time, in such affliction as rendered her careless of surrounding objects. She saw only that he was quiet and unobtrusive, and she liked him for it. He did not disturb the wretchedness of her mind by ill-timed conversation. She was first called to observe and approve him farther, by a reflection which Elinor chanced one day to make on the difference between him and his sister. It was a contrast which recommended him most forcibly to her mother.

"It is enough," said she; "to say that he is unlike Fanny is enough. It implies everything amiable. I love him already."

"I think you will like him," said Elinor, "when you know more of him."

"Like him!" replied her mother with a smile. "I feel no sentiment of approbation inferior to love."

"You may esteem him."

"I have never yet known what it was to separate esteem and love."

—Sense and Sensibility

Elinor and her mother are discussing Edward's character, which gratifies both women. "To say that he is unlike Fanny is enough," Mrs. Dashwood tells her daughter with satisfaction. "It implies everything amiable. I love him already."

But Elinor urges her mother to look beyond this faulty comparison and really get to *know* Edward: "You will like him. . . . *You may esteem him.*"

As one of the prevailing themes in *Sense and Sensibility*—and indeed, in many of Austen's novels—*esteem* means to value as precious, to hold in high regard, to bear sincere and genuine respect toward. Interestingly, Mrs. Dashwood sees no real difference between *love* and *esteem*—they are synonymous to her. She readily equates her affection for Edward with a ready-made esteem, much as a modern-day reader might substitute the word *like* for *love*.

So then, what exactly does it mean to esteem? To Elinor, the definition is obvious. While love is about mutual and binding affection, esteem is the high regard that comes with earning a place of respect in another's heart. By urging her mother to "esteem" Edward, Elinor is hinting that Edward's honorable character has already earned her own respect.

We find the biblical counterpart to this notion in Ephesians 5:2, where we are commanded to "walk in love, [esteeming and delighting in one another] *as Christ loved us and gave Himself up for us*, a slain offering and sacrifice to God [for you, so that it became] a sweet fragrance" (AMP, emphasis added). As a way to mimic Christ's example, "esteeming and delighting" in each other allows us to mirror the way He loved us and to reflect back to one another the sacrifices He made on our behalf.

Do you genuinely esteem those around you, as Christ calls you to do? Or are you driven by emotional and circumstantial whims? Consider Christ's example—and then choose to esteem.

❧

LET NOTHING BE DONE THROUGH SELFISH AMBITION
OR CONCEIT, BUT IN LOWLINESS OF MIND LET EACH
ESTEEM OTHERS BETTER THAN HIMSELF.

Philippians 2:3 NKJV

EVALUATING YOUR FOCUS

"Pride," observed Mary, who piqued herself upon the solidity of her reflections, "is a very common failing I believe. By all that I have ever read, I am convinced that it is very common indeed, that human nature is particularly prone to it, and that there are very few of us who do not cherish a feeling of self-complacency on the score of some quality or other, real or imaginary. Vanity and pride are different things, though the words are often used synonimously. A person may be proud without being vain. Pride relates more to our opinion of ourselves, vanity to what we would have others think of us."

"If I were as rich as Mr. Darcy," cried a young Lucas who came with his sisters, "I should not care how proud I was. I would keep a pack of foxhounds, and drink a bottle of wine every day."

"Then you would drink a great deal more than you ought," said Mrs. Bennet; "and if I were to see you at it, I should take away your bottle directly."

—Pride and Prejudice

According to Mary, pride and vanity are not the same thing, but they *are* closely related: "A person may be proud without being vain. Pride relates more to our opinion of our ourselves, vanity to what we would have others think of us."

To have pride without sin is certainly possible—for example, one can be proud of accomplishing a goal or finishing a project without having a puffed-up ego. However, it is undeniable that at their core, both pride and vanity are *self-*focused. As relates to Mr. Darcy, this is particularly true. His unwillingness to move beyond his social circle—the refusal to introduce himself to new acquaintances at the ball, or to dance with young ladies who have no partners—is evidence that his own personal comfort is his primary goal.

Unfortunately, our society often promotes proud people and gives them great riches, but this nearly always leads the heart *away* from God: "The wicked in his proud countenance does not seek God; God is in none of his thoughts" (Psalm 10:4 NKJV). Perhaps it is because pride is the root of every sin. Pride led Lucifer to rebel against God; pride caused Adam and Eve to disobey God's rules; pride caused King David to lust after what was not his; pride led Judas to betray his Master. The only person in history who ever lived free from pride is Jesus.

Where is your focus? Do you live for making yourself happy, or do you seek to make God happy? Even as you seek after God's heart, you may still struggle with pride because as a Christian, you are still being transformed. However, you can be certain that *His* way of living is richer, freer, and more abundant than your own.

❧

COMMAND THOSE WHO ARE RICH IN THIS PRESENT AGE
NOT TO BE HAUGHTY, NOR TO TRUST IN UNCERTAIN
RICHES BUT IN THE LIVING GOD, WHO GIVES US
RICHLY ALL THINGS TO ENJOY.

1 Timothy 6:17 NKJV

SPIRITUAL BANKRUPTCY

"If we can persuade your father to all this," said Lady Russell, looking over her paper, "much may be done. If he will adopt these regulations, in seven years he will be clear; and I hope we may be able to convince him and Eliza-beth, that Kellynch Hall has a respectability in itself which cannot be affected by these reductions; and that the true dignity of Sir Walter Elliot will be very far from lessened in the eyes of sensible people, by acting like a man of prin-ciple. What will he be doing, in fact, but what very many of our first families have done, or ought to do? There will be nothing singular in his case; and it is singularity which often makes the worst part of our suffering, as it always does of our conduct. I have great hope of prevailing. We must be serious and decided; for after all, the person who has contracted debts must pay them; and though a great deal is due to the feelings of the gentleman, and the head of a house, like your father, there is still more due to the character of an hon-est man."

This was the principle on which Anne wanted her father to be proceed-ing, his friends to be urging him. She considered it as an act of indispensable duty to clear away the claims of creditors with all the expedition which the most comprehensive retrenchments could secure, and saw no dignity in any-thing short of it. She wanted it to be prescribed, and felt as a duty.

—Persuasion

In Jane Austen's day, paying off one's debt was a matter of principle, no matter how much it meant economizing. As *Persuasion* opens, we see that Sir Walter's extravagant spending habits have led him to seek advice regarding his financial straits. Lady Russell and Sir Walter's pragmatic middle daughter, Anne, draw up a plan for economizing, on the principle that "the person who has contracted debts must pay them."

In today's economy, many are being driven to bankruptcy—essentially, the "forgiveness" of accrued debt. Interestingly, bankruptcy carries a seven-year judgment that has roots in Scripture: "At the end of every seventh year you must cancel the debts of everyone who owes you money" (Deuteronomy 15:1 NLT). This seven-year mandate contains an important spiritual parallel: while the law of justice demands repayment for monies borrowed, the law of mercy extends grace if this is impossible. Through bankruptcy, it is possible for debtors to obtain forgiveness and receive a fresh start.

Economic bankruptcy offers just a tiny glimpse of the forgiveness that we experience through Jesus' sacrifice for us. When we acknowledge that we are spiritually bankrupt and that our debt is too great to repay, He offers us the greatest "fresh start" we could imagine. The debt has *already* been canceled.

If you are in over your head financially, like Sir Walter, confess your circumstances to God and ask for His wisdom and guidance in moving forward. Then stop for a moment to appreciate something significant: for every debt, someone must pay. Jesus, by His grace and mercy, offers each of us a fresh start.

❦

"Two men were in debt to a banker. One owed five hundred silver pieces, the other fifty. Neither of them could pay up, and so the banker canceled both debts. Which of the two would be more grateful?"

Luke 7:42 MSG

RESPECTING ONE ANOTHER

Emma was not sorry to be pressed. She read, and was surprized. The style of the letter was much above her expectation. There were not merely no grammatical errors, but as a composition it would not have disgraced a gentleman; the language, though plain, was strong and unaffected, and the sentiments it conveyed very much to the credit of the writer. It was short, but expressed good sense, warm attachment, liberality, propriety, even delicacy of feeling. She paused over it, while Harriet stood anxiously watching for her opinion, with a "Well, well," and was at last forced to add, "Is it a good letter? or is it too short?"

"Yes, indeed, a very good letter," replied Emma rather slowly—"so good a letter, Harriet, that every thing considered, I think one of his sisters must have helped him. I can hardly imagine the young man whom I saw talking with you the other day could express himself so well, if left quite to his own powers, and yet it is not the style of a woman; no, certainly, it is too strong and concise; not diffuse enough for a woman. No doubt he is a sensible man, and I suppose may have a natural talent for—thinks strongly and clearly—and when he takes a pen in hand, his thoughts naturally find proper words. It is so with some men. Yes, I understand the sort of mind. Vigorous, decided, with sentiments to a certain point, not coarse. A better written letter, Harriet (returning it,) than I had expected."

—Emma

In Emma's world of social and class barriers, there are haves and have-nots. And Mr. Martin—by virtue of being a farmer—is a have-not. It is thus unsurprising that when Harriet shows Emma the warm, eloquent, and thoughtfully worded letter that has just come from Mr. Martin, Emma is "surprised [because] the style of the letter was much above her expectation." Her pride has received a blow: she can hardly believe that a man she deems her inferior in every way could craft a letter equal in quality to something that might flow from the pen of a gentleman.

In Romans 13:7, Paul instructs the Roman Christians to "pay to all what is owed to them; taxes to whom taxes are owed, revenue to whom revenue is owed, respect to whom respect is owed, honor to whom honor is owed."

Paul's instruction is not just about submitting to civil authority; it is also a call for Christ's followers to begin acting and living with the respect and honor toward one another that God commands, and that Christ set the example for. When we label or judge one another by appearance, performance, or material possessions, we are not just resisting an important scriptural command; we are rebelling against God in our hearts.

Like Emma, are you guilty of dismissing others as lower than yourself? Next time you are tempted to overlook someone you secretly deem inferior, consider that you are missing an opportunity to show Christ's love and obey His commands. Ask God to soften your heart and fill it with His perfect love and respect.

ᕕᕗ

HONOR ALL PEOPLE, LOVE THE FAMILY OF BELIEVERS,
FEAR GOD, HONOR THE KING.

1 Peter 2:17 NET

Letting Christ Be Your Guide

"But, aunt, [Fanny] is really so very ignorant!"

"Very true indeed, [Maria and Julia], but you are blessed with wonderful memories, and your poor cousin has probably none at all. There is a vast deal of difference in memories, as well as in everything else, and therefore you must make allowance for your cousin, and pity her deficiency. And remember that, if you are ever so forward and clever yourselves, you should always be modest; for, much as you know already, there is a great deal more for you to learn."

"Yes, I know there is, till I am seventeen. But I must tell you another thing of Fanny, so odd and so stupid. Do you know, she says she does not want to learn either music or drawing."

"To be sure, my dear, that is very stupid indeed, and shows a great want of genius and emulation. But, all things considered, I do not know whether it is not as well that it should be so, for, though you know (owing to me) your papa and mama are so good as to bring her up with you, it is not at all necessary that she should be as accomplished as you are;—on the contrary, it is much more desirable that there should be a difference."

Such were the counsels by which Mrs. Norris assisted to form her nieces' minds; and it is not very wonderful that, with all their promising talents and early information, they should be entirely deficient in the less common acquirements of self-knowledge, generosity and humility. In everything but disposition they were admirably taught.

—*Mansfield Park*

In this scene, sisters Maria and Julia Bertram are complaining to their aunt Norris about their cousin Fanny's lack of book knowledge. Their aunt laughingly agrees that Fanny is "very stupid indeed," but adds cheerfully that Fanny should *not* be so accomplished as the Bertram girls; she is of a lower class. Aunt Norris is effectively approving the cousins' harsh judgment that Fanny does not deserve to be educated like they are.

God has put within each of us a need for approval. Sometimes we look for it from sources like Mrs. Norris—people we look up to and who tell us what we want to hear, who soothe our ruffled feelings, who reassure us in ways that grow our vanity. This is a mistake, and Proverbs 29:25 tells us why: "The fear of man lays a snare, but whoever trusts in the LORD is safe." If we let this sort of shallow opinion guide our impulses and shape our dispositions, it will only deepen our need for acceptance—and we will ultimately seek the wrong people to fill it, just as Maria and Julia eventually do.

Our desire for acceptance is a craving that no one but God Himself can fill . . . and already has: Christ bought us the gift of salvation. Could we trust anyone more than the One who paid for our forgiveness with His life?

⚜

How blessed is God! . . . Long, long ago he decided to adopt us into his family through Jesus Christ. (What pleasure he took in planning this!) He wanted us to enter into the celebration of his lavish gift-giving by the hand of his beloved Son.

Ephesians 1:3–6 MSG

MEEK AND GENTLE SPIRIT

In the evening, as Marianne was discovered to be musical, she was invited to play [the pianoforte]. The instrument was unlocked, every body prepared to be charmed, and Marianne, who sang very well, at their request, went through the chief of the songs which Lady Middleton had brought into the family on her marriage, and which perhaps had lain ever since in the same position on the pianoforte, for her ladyship had celebrated that event by giving up music. . . .

Marianne's performance was highly applauded. Sir John was loud in his admiration at the end of every song, and as loud in his conversation with the others while every song lasted. Lady Middleton frequently called him to order, wondered how any one's attention could be diverted from music for a moment, and asked Marianne to sing a particular song which Marianne had just finished.

Colonel Brandon alone, of all the party, heard her without being in raptures. He paid her only the compliment of attention, and she felt a respect for him on the occasion, which the other had reasonably forfeited by their shameless want of taste. His pleasure in music, though it amounted not to that ecstatic delight which alone could sympathize with her own, was estimable when contrasted against the horrible insensibility of the others; and she was reasonable enough to allow that a man of five and thirty might well have outlived all acuteness of feeling and every exquisite power of enjoyment. She was perfectly disposed to make every allowance for the colonel's advanced state of life which humanity required.

—*Sense and Sensibility*

ometimes it is only through comparison that we recognize the virtues of a quiet and gentle spirit. Such is the case in this scene, where Colonel Brandon, an "old bachelor . . . on the wrong side of five and thirty," fails to make a strong impression upon the emotionally unrestrained Marianne.

Until she begins to play the pianoforte. At once, the colonel's quiet nature is elevated through the benefit of contrast. Perhaps it is his absence of overwrought dramatic expression, as exemplified by Sir John; more likely, the lack of Lady Middleton's self-aggrandizement or Mrs. Jennings's bawdy expressions. Maybe it is the simple compliment of gentlemanly attention.

Whatever the case, Marianne sees that the colonel's reserved nature sets him apart from the other partygoers. He expresses exactly what he feels, rendering his compliments precious. This Marianne recognizes—perhaps for the first time—as a mark of good taste.

For Christians today, this simple example provides context for the virtues of Spirit-filled living. A gentle and quiet spirit, like Colonel Brandon's, pleases the Lord. Romans 8:14 tells us, "For as many are led by the Spirit of God, these are sons of God" (NKJV). An attention-getting, self-serving person is hardly an example of God-centered living; yet everywhere we look we see individuals clawing their way toward and striving endlessly for attention.

Let your personal manner of expression be a reflection of Christ-centered living, and the things that capture your attention reveal wisdom and tastefulness. The way to ensure this mode of living is to seek your security and your example in Christ.

༄

"TAKE MY YOKE UPON YOU AND LEARN FROM ME,
FOR I AM GENTLE AND HUMBLE IN HEART, AND YOU
WILL FIND REST FOR YOUR SOULS."

Matthew 11:29 NASB

DEVELOPING CONTENTMENT

At five o'clock [Caroline Bingley and Louisa Hurst] retired to dress, and at half past six Elizabeth was summoned to dinner. To the civil enquiries which then poured in, and amongst which she had the pleasure of distinguishing the much superior solicitude of Mr. Bingley's, she could not make a very favourable answer. Jane was by no means better. [Mr. Bingley's] sisters, on hearing this, repeated three or four times how much they were grieved, how shocking it was to have a bad cold, and how excessively they disliked being ill themselves, and then thought no more of the matter; and their indifference towards Jane, when not immediately before them, restored Elizabeth to the enjoyment of all her original dislike.

[Mr. Bingley], indeed, was the only one of the party whom she could regard with any complacency. His anxiety for Jane was evident, and his attentions to herself most pleasing, and they prevented her feeling herself so much an intruder as she believed she was considered by the others. She had very little notice from any but him. Miss Bingley was engrossed by Mr. Darcy, her sister scarcely less so; and as for Mr. Hurst, by whom Elizabeth sat, he was an indolent man, who lived only to eat, drink, and play at cards, who, when he found her prefer a plain dish to a ragout, had nothing to say to her.

—Pride and Prejudice

If Jane were inclined to think ill of anyone, she might do so toward her new so-called friends, Mr. Bingley's sisters. Really, with friends like Miss Bingley and Mrs. Hurst, who needs enemies? But Jane looks for the best in others, and that includes the two ladies at Netherfield.

Elizabeth, however, is not so kindly disposed. In this scene, Lizzy silently observes the ladies' "indifference towards Jane, when not immediately before them," and is justifiably offended on her sister's behalf. Lizzy recognizes that their concern is a pretense and their interests purely self-centered, and she is restored in feeling to "all her original dislike."

Jealousy, as we see, rips apart friendships and pits people against one another. It manifests itself frequently through biting words and cutting remarks. In this case, it masquerades as concern but seeks to tear down.

The shepherd David experienced a similar betrayal. After David killed the Philistine Goliath for the Israelite army, he was met back home with a parade and great acclaim. His fans lined the streets, crying, "Saul has struck down his thousands, and David his ten thousands" (1 Samuel 18:7). David's former ally, King Saul, was consumed by jealousy from that day forward: "The next day a harmful spirit from God rushed upon Saul, and he raved within his house while David was playing the lyre, as he did day by day. Saul had his spear in his hand. And Saul hurled the spear, for he thought, 'I will pin David to the wall'" (vv. 10–11). The sinful choices made by a jealous heart carry great potential for destruction.

God can help you eliminate the weeds of jealousy in your life and replace them with joy and thankfulness; this is accomplished by seeking contentment in His provision alone. Give God whatever is bothering you and ask Him to take care of it. Draw near to Him . . . and He will draw near to you.

❦

I HAVE LEARNED IN WHATEVER SITUATION I AM TO BE CONTENT. I KNOW HOW TO BE BROUGHT LOW, AND I KNOW HOW TO ABOUND.

Philippians 4:11–12

When Teasing Is Lying

"You do not really think, Mr. Thorpe," said Catherine, venturing after some time to consider the matter as entirely decided, and to offer some little variation on the subject, *"that James's gig will break down?"*

"Break down! Oh! Lord! Did you ever see such a little tittuppy thing in your life? There is not a sound piece of iron about it . . . I would not be bound to go two miles in it for fifty thousand pounds."

"Good heavens!" cried Catherine, quite frightened. *"Then pray . . . do let us turn back, Mr. Thorpe; stop and speak to my brother, and tell him how very unsafe it is."*

"Unsafe! Oh, lord! What is there in that? They will only get a roll if it does break down; and there is plenty of dirt; it will be excellent falling. Oh, curse it! The carriage is safe enough, if a man knows how to drive it; a thing of that sort in good hands will last above twenty years after it is fairly worn out. Lord bless you! I would undertake for five pounds to drive it to York and back again, without losing a nail."

Catherine listened with astonishment; she knew not how to reconcile two such very different accounts of the same thing; for she had not been brought up to understand the propensities of a rattle, nor to know to how many idle assertions and impudent falsehoods the excess of vanity will lead. Her own family were plain, matter-of-fact people who seldom aimed at wit of any kind; her father, at the utmost, being contented with a pun, and her mother with a proverb; they were not in the habit therefore of telling lies to increase their importance, or of asserting at one moment what they would contradict the next.

—*Northanger Abbey*

Though Jane Austen is somewhat poking fun at Catherine's naïveté, this scene reveals the real danger lurking behind John Thorpe's demeanor: he is a man given to "idle assertions, impudent falsehoods, and an excess of vanity, with the aim of increasing his importance and contradicting himself to fluster his audience." In other words, he likes to stir up trouble, and he does it with a tease—in his case, a dressed-up lie.

In short, John embodies what the Bible calls "double-tongued" (1 Timothy 3:8). His favorite type of teasing—namely, saying one thing and contradicting it moments later—is not centered on enjoying a good, wholesome time with his friends or promoting goodwill; rather, it is an avenue to boast about himself, a means of putting people down and making them feel uncomfortable, a way to disrespect and embarrass others through hurtful and thoughtless words. Worst of all, he protests afterward that it is all "in fun." But fun for whom? Is his habit born out of a desire to love and serve others, as Christ commands? Or is it a by-product of "jealousy and selfish ambition" (James 3:16)?

Think about this carefully. Do your teasing words ever come at the cost of someone else's discomfort? Does your sarcastic wit sometimes hurt a friend, a spouse, or a parent? Unless God guides your hearts *and* your words, your tongue can be a destructive weapon that tears down rather than builds up.

ஒஒ

THE WISDOM THAT IS FROM ABOVE IS FIRST PURE,
THEN PEACEABLE, GENTLE, AND EASY TO BE
INTREATED, FULL OF MERCY AND GOOD FRUITS,
WITHOUT PARTIALITY, AND WITHOUT HYPOCRISY.

James 3:17 KJV

STIRRING UP TROUBLE

When dinner was over, [Lizzy] returned directly to Jane, and Miss Bingley began abusing her as soon as she was out of the room. Her manners were pronounced to be very bad indeed, a mixture of pride and impertinence; she had no conversation, no stile, no taste, no beauty. Mrs. Hurst thought the same, and added,

"She has nothing, in short, to recommend her, but being an excellent walker. I shall never forget her appearance this morning. She really looked almost wild."

"She did indeed, Louisa. I could hardly keep my countenance. Very nonsensical to come at all! Why must she be scampering about the country, because her sister had a cold? Her hair so untidy, so blowsy!"

"Yes, and her petticoat; I hope you saw her petticoat, six inches deep in mud, I am absolutely certain; and the gown which had been let down to hide it not doing its office."

"Your picture may be very exact, Louisa," said Bingley; "but this was all lost upon me. I thought Miss Elizabeth Bennet looked remarkably well, when she came into the room this morning. Her dirty petticoat quite escaped my notice."

"You observed it, Mr. Darcy, I am sure," said Miss Bingley, "and I am inclined to think that you would not wish to see your sister make such an exhibition."

"Certainly not."

"To walk three miles, or four miles, or five miles, or whatever it is, above her ancles in dirt, and alone, quite alone! what could she mean by it? It seems to me to shew an abominable sort of conceited independence, a most country town indifference to decorum."

—Pride and Prejudice

Ugly words fly in this scene, as Mr. Bingley's sisters seize the opportunity to make fun of Elizabeth the moment she leaves the room. But their plan backfires: the ridiculous picture they paint of Lizzy creates in Darcy a growing appreciation for her "conceited independence." Perhaps it is because it demonstrates that Lizzy does not care about the opinions of silly people. Or perhaps it underscores how strikingly different she is from the double-tongued young ladies prattling at him.

In Romans 1, the apostle Paul speaks severely about the kind of discord Miss Bingley is sowing: "They were filled with all manner of unrighteousness. . . . They are gossips, slanderers, haters of God, insolent, haughty, boastful, inventors of evil, disobedient to parents, foolish, faithless, heartless, ruthless. Though they know God's decree that those who practice such things deserve to die, they not only do them but give approval to those who practice them" (vv. 29–32).

Paul places *gossips* and *slanderers* into the same category as *God-haters* and *murderers*! This is because backstabbing is more than a nasty little habit; every time we let ourselves indulge, our hearts grow a little hardened to sin and less sensitive to the Spirit's leading.

If you struggle to keep from talking about others or spreading rumors, confess it to the Lord. Ask Him to be the guide of your tongue, your thoughts, and your actions.

⁂

I WILL WATCH MY WAYS AND
KEEP MY TONGUE FROM SIN;
I WILL PUT A MUZZLE ON MY MOUTH
AS LONG AS THE WICKED ARE IN MY PRESENCE.

Psalm 39:1 NIV

LOVING LIKE JESUS

"Not Harriet's equal!" exclaimed Mr. Knightley loudly and warmly; and with calmer asperity, added, a few moments afterwards, "No, he is not her equal indeed, for he is as much her superior in sense as in situation. Emma, your infatuation about that girl blinds you. What are Harriet Smith's claims, either of birth, nature or education, to any connexion higher than Robert Martin? She is the natural daughter of nobody knows whom, with probably no settled provision at all, and certainly no respectable relations. She is known only as parlour-boarder at a common school. She is not a sensible girl, nor a girl of any information. She has been taught nothing useful, and is too young and too simple to have acquired any thing herself. At her age she can have no experience, and with her little wit, is not very likely ever to have any that can avail her. She is pretty, and she is good tempered, and that is all. My only scruple in advising the match was on his account, as being beneath his deserts, and a bad connexion for him. I felt that, as to fortune, in all probability he might do much better; and that as to a rational companion or useful helpmate, he could not do worse. But I could not reason so to a man in love, and was willing to trust to there being no harm in her, to her having that sort of disposition, which, in good hands, like his, might be easily led aright and turn out very well. The advantage of the match I felt to be all on her side."

—Emma

Poor Mr. Martin. At no point in *Emma* do we get to hear him speak up and defend himself; yet he remains one of the most-discussed minor characters in Austen's writing. Harriet, Mr. Knightley, even Mrs. Weston—all chime in with their benign opinions of Mr. Martin. In short, it seems, everyone thinks highly of him . . . except Emma.

When Mr. Knightley points out drawbacks to Harriet's circumstances—poor education and lack of more suitable prospects, for example—Emma implies that her own influence and connections will more than compensate.

That Emma is blind to Mr. Martin's good qualities is unsurprising, for she is equally blind to her dear friend Harriet's flaws. This "partiality" toward Harriet is not born out of natural goodwill or pure affection, but a self-important desire for Emma to see her protégé elevated. In other words, Emma's self-importance is being projected onto Harriet in the name of loyalty and friendship.

This is just the kind of self-love that we are advised *against* in 1 Corinthians 13:4–5: "Love . . . does not act unbecomingly; it does not seek its own" (NASB). If Emma were putting Harriet's needs first, she would recognize the honor and blessing in being loved by Mr. Martin. Mr. Knightley sees it, but Emma is stubborn—and selfish.

Love that gives generously and acts becomingly, that does not put self first: it is the example we strive to emulate, if we would follow Jesus.

❧

For by grace you have been saved through faith. And this is not your own doing; it is the gift of God, not a result of works, so that no one may boast.

Ephesians 2:8–9

TRUE LOVE'S ENDURANCE

Once, and once only, in the course of many years, had [Fanny] the happiness of being with [her brother] William. Of the rest she saw nothing: nobody seemed to think of her ever going amongst them again, even for a visit, nobody at home seemed to want her; but William determining, soon after her removal, to be a sailor, was invited to spend a week with his sister in Northamptonshire before he went to sea. Their eager affection in meeting, their exquisite delight in being together, their hours of happy mirth, and moments of serious conference, may be imagined; as well as the sanguine views and spirits of the boy even to the last, and the misery of the girl when he left her. Luckily the visit happened in the Christmas holidays, when she could directly look for comfort to her cousin Edmund; and he told her such charming things of what William was to do, and be hereafter, in consequence of his profession, as made her gradually admit that the separation might have some use. Edmund's friendship never failed her: his leaving Eton for Oxford made no change in his kind dispositions, and only afforded more frequent opportunities of proving them. Without any display of doing more than the rest, or any fear of doing too much, he was always true to her interests, and considerate of her feelings, trying to make her good qualities understood, and to conquer the diffidence which prevented their being more apparent; giving her advice, consolation, and encouragement.

—Mansfield Park

In this scene, we get a glimpse of the purest, deepest love: from Fanny's devoted brother William, now gone to sea; and from her kind cousin Edmund, whose friendship has "never failed her." Fanny is infinitely and eternally grateful for the love she receives, and she loves these two men faithfully in return.

This picture of true love, given and received, is best examined in 1 Corinthians 13, the Bible's famous "love chapter." Within the first few verses, Paul makes very clear that Christianity without love is nothing: "If I speak in the tongues of men and of angels, but have not love, I am a noisy gong or a clanging cymbal. And if I have prophetic powers, and understand all mysteries and all knowledge, and if I have all faith, so as to remove mountains, but have not love, I am nothing. If I give away all I have, and if I deliver up my body to be burned, but have not love, I gain nothing" (vv. 1–3). What Paul means is that no matter how good our performance or appearance or even our faith, lack of love deflates it entirely.

So often, love is misunderstood and distorted by an unbelieving world. We accept shallow substitutions and celebrate them as though they were real or lasting. What we fail to grasp is that Christian love is a choice first demonstrated toward us by God, and that we get to practice it ourselves as we follow Him and little by little become like Him . . . as we become like Love. What a beautiful picture of love we have in God!

᠅

WHOEVER DOES NOT LOVE DOES NOT KNOW GOD,
BECAUSE GOD IS LOVE.

1 John 4:8 NIV

DEVELOPING SELF-CONTROL

"Mamma," said Marianne . . . "I am sure Edward Ferrars is not well. We have now been here almost a fortnight, and yet he does not come. Nothing but real indisposition could occasion this extraordinary delay. What else can detain him at Norland?"

"Had you any idea of his coming so soon?" said Mrs. Dashwood. "I had none. On the contrary, if I have felt any anxiety at all on the subject, it has been in recollecting that he sometimes showed a want of pleasure and readiness in accepting my invitation, when I talked of his coming to Baron. Does Elinor expect him already?"

"I have never mentioned it to her, but of course she must."

"I rather think you are mistaken, for when I was talking to her yesterday of getting a new grate for the spare bedchamber, she observed that there was no immediate hurry for it, as it was not likely that the room would be wanted for some time."

"How strange this is! What can be the meaning of it! But the whole of their behaviour to each other has been unaccountable! How cold, how composed were their last adieus! How languid their conversation the last evening of their being together! In Edward's farewell there was no distinction between Elinor and me: it was the good wishes of an affectionate brother to both."

—Sense and Sensibility

Two sisters: one decorous and reserved, the other given to fancy and spontaneity. Each personifies one of the eponymous themes. Will the innate nature of one prove advantageous? Time will tell.

In this particular scene, a conversation between mother and daughter offers readers a glimpse at how young Marianne views elder sister Elinor's self-control in matters of love. Marianne thinks love best conveyed as an emotional outpouring; to her, Elinor's propriety toward Edward signifies a failure to experience love in its full state.

Scriptures abounds with examples mirroring Marianne's signature freedom of expression. The psalmist David, for example, expresses the heights and depths of his feelings in themes ranging from lament to praise, anguish to thanksgiving. Certainly all are God-given emotions, and as such are to be celebrated.

But there is a second consideration. In 2 Peter, we are instructed to "make every effort to supplement your faith with virtue, and virtue with knowledge, and knowledge with self-control, and self-control with steadfastness, and steadfastness with godliness, and godliness with brotherly affection, and brotherly affection with love" (1:5–7). In this admonishment, we see that self-control is equal to love, virtue, knowledge, and godliness—a necessary element in the God-ordained progression of character development.

Are you by nature spontaneous and irrepressible, or do you tend more toward guarding your heart and practicing the discipline of self-control? Yes, all of our emotions are gifts from God; but if moderation in any area is lacking, it can prove disastrous. Examine your heart and ask God to reveal what areas He might work in you to develop your character.

❦

BUT THE FRUIT OF THE SPIRIT IS LOVE, JOY, PEACE, LONGSUFFERING, KINDNESS, GOODNESS, FAITHFULNESS, GENTLENESS, SELF-CONTROL.

Galatians 5:22–23 NKJV

"Being" in Jesus' Presence

Had she found Jane in any apparent danger, Mrs. Bennet would have been very miserable; but being satisfied on seeing her, that her illness was not alarming, she had no wish of her recovering immediately, as her restoration to health would probably remove her from Netherfield. She would not listen therefore to her daughter's proposal of being carried home. . . .

After sitting a little while with Jane, on Miss Bingley's appearance and invitation the mother and three daughters all attended her into the breakfast parlour. Bingley met them with hopes that Mrs. Bennet had not found Miss Bennet worse than she expected.

"Indeed I have, Sir," was her answer. "She is a great deal too ill to be moved. Mr. Jones says we must not think of moving her. We must trespass a little longer on your kindness."

"Removed!" cried Bingley. "It must not be thought of. My sister, I am sure, will not hear of her removal."

"You may depend upon it, Madam," said Miss Bingley, with cold civility, "that Miss Bennet shall receive every possible attention while she remains with us."

Mrs. Bennet was profuse in her acknowledgments.

"I am sure," she added, "if it was not for such good friends I do not know what would become of her, for she is very ill indeed, and suffers a vast deal, though with the greatest patience in the world—which is always the way with her, for she has, without exception, the sweetest temper I ever met with. I often tell my other girls they are nothing to her."

—*Pride and Prejudice*

Since the moment they met, Jane has been enchanting Mr. Bingley with her sweet, demure manner. But Mrs. Bennet, unaware of the growing attachment between the two, takes it upon herself to praise Jane to the world at large, and to Mr. Bingley in particular. Her ulterior motive—to marry her daughter to a wealthy landowner—is obvious to everyone.

Having a motive is not necessarily wrong. Sometimes it spurs us on to achieve great things. In Mrs. Bingley's case, for example, the motive to match Jane with Mr. Bingley springs from a wish to ensure her daughter's provision. However, she also wants to elevate her own status and enjoy a wealthy lifestyle, and here—in selfishness—is where her motive becomes flawed.

A biblical example of impure motive is found in Luke 10, when Jesus and His disciples stop at Mary and Martha's home for some refreshment. Mary ends up sitting at Jesus' feet, listening to Him speak; meanwhile, Martha—wanting to be the perfect hostess—frantically tries to get everything together.

Pretty soon, Martha realizes she is doing all the hard work while Mary enjoys the company of their Lord! Martha's ulterior motive, it turns out, is be recognized and appreciated, which eclipses her hard work and robs her of the joy of being in Jesus' presence.

If you sense that your purpose for doing something has gotten off track, ask the Lord for His discernment. Take time to evaluate your heart motive in how you allocate your time. Remember, sometimes doing for others is not as important as simply being present with the Savior.

❧

WHETHER THEREFORE YE EAT, OR DRINK, OR WHATSOEVER
YE DO, DO ALL TO THE GLORY OF GOD.

1 Corinthians 10:31 KJV

SEEKING GOD'S COUNSEL

Elizabeth had been lately forming an intimacy, which [Lady Russell] wished to see interrupted. It was with the daughter of Mr Shepherd, who had returned, after an unprosperous marriage, to her father's house, with the additional burden of two children. She was a clever young woman, who understood the art of pleasing—the art of pleasing, at least, at Kellynch Hall; and who had made herself so acceptable to Miss Elliot, as to have been already staying there more than once, in spite of all that Lady Russell, who thought it a friendship quite out of place, could hint of caution and reserve.

Lady Russell, indeed, had scarcely any influence with Elizabeth, and seemed to love her, rather because she would love her, than because Elizabeth deserved it. She had never received from her more than outward attention, nothing beyond the observances of complaisance; had never succeeded in any point which she wanted to carry, against previous inclination. She had been repeatedly very earnest in trying to get Anne included in the visit to London, sensibly open to all the injustice and all the discredit of the selfish arrangements which shut her out, and on many lesser occasions had endeavoured to give Elizabeth the advantage of her own better judgement and experience; but always in vain: Elizabeth would go her own way; and never had she pursued it in more decided opposition to Lady Russell than in this selection of Mrs Clay; turning from the society of so deserving a sister, to bestow her affection and confidence on one who ought to have been nothing to her but the object of distant civility.

—*Persuasion*

ady Russell highly disapproves of Elizabeth's strong attachment to Mrs. Clay, a coy young divorcee who "understood the art of pleasing . . . at least, at Kellynch Hall." What breaks Lady Russell's heart even more is seeing Elizabeth's affection for Mrs. Clay supplant Elizabeth's loyalty to her own dear sister, Anne. But Elizabeth's choices often oppose Lady Russell's advice; this is nothing new. And Elizabeth has inherited just enough of her father's vanity that she will keep the company of whomever she likes, despite the consequences.

From its opening words, the book of Proverbs encourages us not to make decisions before seeking wise counsel, in order "to know wisdom and instruction, to discern the sayings of understanding, to receive instruction in wise behavior, righteousness, justice and equity; to give prudence to the naive" (1:2–4 NASB). While seeking wise counsel is a God-given source of protection and accountability, it is not foolproof. We see this clearly in the example of Lady Russell's persuading Anne, seven years earlier, to break off her romance with the poor naval officer Captain Wentworth. Anne meekly took Lady Russell's advice and has never recovered from her broken heart.

This reminder is further proof that the only error-free road to wisdom is found in asking for and following God's guidance above all others'. A wise person will listen to and heed godly counsel from contemporaries, but not before beseeching God to lead the way and choosing to trust His outcome.

Do you seek God's wisdom even before you ask the opinion of your most godly, God-fearing friends? He wants us to surround ourselves with wise mentors who can help safeguard and protect us, but even more than that, He wants us to seek His face and obey His Word.

❧

THE FEAR OF THE LORD IS THE BEGINNING OF KNOWLEDGE.

Proverbs 1:7 NASB

A CRITICAL SPIRIT

[Mary Crawford:] "Ay, you have been brought up to it. It was no part of my education; and the only dose I ever had, being administered by not the first favourite in the world, has made me consider improvements as the greatest of nuisances. Three years ago the Admiral, my honoured uncle, bought a cottage at Twickenham for us all to spend our summers in; and my aunt and I went down to it quite in raptures; but it being excessively pretty, it was soon found necessary to be improved, and for three months we were all dirt and confusion, without a gravel walk to step on, or a bench fit for use. I would have everything as complete as possible in the country, shrubberies and flower-gardens, and rustic seats innumerable: but it must all be done without my care. Henry is different; he loves to be doing."

Edmund was sorry to hear Miss Crawford, whom he was much disposed to admire, speak so freely of her uncle. It did not suit his sense of propriety, and he was silenced, till induced by further smiles and liveliness to put the matter by for the present.

—Mansfield Park

erein lies an early hint of Mary Crawford's critical spirit. Her quickness to speak harshly of her uncle, the Admiral, reveals her quick-to-judge nature—a failing that does not escape Edmund's notice, even though he is already disposed to think the best about Mary.

A critical spirit tears others down in order to build oneself up. In Mary, this habit is seen over and over, though no one but Fanny seems to be aware of it. This is because Mary makes full use of disarming devices—laughter, pretty speeches, and lively chatter—that charm her listeners into thinking her cattiness innocent. Fanny alone sees the danger, and worries for Edmund's heart.

Make no mistake: when we judge others and voice those opinions, it is borne of self interest—we want to feel better about ourselves. But the Bible makes very clear that God alone holds the right to judgment: "Who are you to pass judgment on the servant of another? It is before his own master that he stands or falls" (Romans 14:4). When we let criticism pass our lips, we're choosing to play God in a way that does not honor Him or invite His Spirit to work in our lives.

Next time a harsh criticism comes to your mind, defuse it in this way: by recalling the grace you have been shown—and that you have been spared through Christ. Choose to think and speak words of mercy instead, just as God chose to demonstrate toward you.

❧

"JUDGE NOT, THAT YOU BE NOT JUDGED."

Matthew 7:1

HONORING YOUR PARENTS

Mr. John Knightley . . . was not a great favourite with his fair sister-in-law. Nothing wrong in him escaped her. She was quick in feeling the little injuries to Isabella, which Isabella never felt herself. Perhaps she might have passed over more had his manners been flattering to Isabella's sister, but they were only those of a calmly kind brother and friend, without praise and without blindness; but hardly any degree of personal compliment could have made her regardless of that greatest fault of all in her eyes which he sometimes fell into, the want of respectful forbearance towards her father. There he had not always the patience that could have been wished. Mr. Woodhouse's peculiarities and fidgetiness were sometimes provoking him to a rational remonstrance or sharp retort equally ill-bestowed. It did not often happen; for Mr. John Knightley had really a great regard for his father-in-law, and generally a strong sense of what was due to him; but it was too often for Emma's charity, especially as there was all the pain of apprehension frequently to be endured, though the offence came not. The beginning, however, of every visit displayed none but the properest feelings, and this being of necessity so short might be hoped to pass away in unsullied cordiality. They had not been long seated and composed when Mr. Woodhouse, with a melancholy shake of the head and a sigh, called his daughter's attention to the sad change at Hartfield since she had been there last.

—Emma

One of Emma's best-loved qualities is the deep loyalty she feels toward her father, Mr. Henry Woodhouse. He is a funny character—prone to anxiety and with a deep mistrust of anything that might threaten his health or lifestyle, including rich food, damp evenings, and potential betrothals. His speeches are filled with allusions to "Poor Miss Taylor" and "Poor Isabella"—two women who have gone on to live lives away from Highbury, with their husbands.

Mr. Woodhouse may be a hypochondriac who always fusses over trifling matters, but he is also benevolent, generous, and hospitable. These are the qualities that Emma loves; she would go to great lengths to prevent hurting his feelings or causing him a moment's unrest.

This explains Emma's single grievance with her brother-in-law, John Knightley: he displays the occasional "want of respectful forbearance towards her father." To Emma, it is unacceptable that anyone's behavior toward her father lack the full courtesy he is due.

What we see in this fierce display of loyalty is that daughter Emma takes seriously the fifth commandment: "Honor your father and your mother, that your days may be long in the land that the LORD your God is giving you" (Exodus 20:12). This kind of honor is a redemptive quality in Emma. She may be selfish in many ways, but her attitude of respect toward her father is pure: not dependent on circumstance, or her own interests, or the approval of others.

Do you choose to honor your parents or other authority figures that God has put into your life? Or do you sometimes struggle to respect them because you find them ridiculous, or overbearing, or frustrating? Next time you are tempted to retort or reprove, remember that honoring your parents is not just about how we treat them; it is a glimpse of how much we respect God.

❧

HONOR ALL PEOPLE, LOVE THE FAMILY OF BELIEVERS,
FEAR GOD, HONOR THE KING.

1 Peter 2:17 NET

BAITING

Miss Bingley saw, or suspected, enough to be jealous; and her great anxiety for the recovery of her dear friend Jane received some assistance from her desire of getting rid of Elizabeth.

She often tried to provoke Darcy into disliking her guest, by talking of their supposed marriage, and planning his happiness in such an alliance.

"I hope," said she, as they were walking together in the shrubbery the next day, "you will give your mother-in-law a few hints, when this desirable event takes place, as to the advantage of holding her tongue; and if you can compass it, do cure the younger girls of running after the officers.—And, if I may mention so delicate a subject, endeavour to check that little something, bordering on conceit and impertinence, which your lady possesses."

"Have you any thing else to propose for my domestic felicity?"

"Oh! yes.—Do let the portraits of your uncle and aunt Philips be placed in the gallery at Pemberley. Put them next to your great uncle, the judge. They are in the same profession, you know; only in different lines. As for your Elizabeth's picture, you must not attempt to have it taken, for what painter could do justice to those beautiful eyes?"

—Pride and Prejudice

aroline Bingley may be a snobby, manipulative young lady, but she is also extremely perceptive—and she strongly suspects that Mr. Darcy is falling in love with Elizabeth. Because she wants Darcy for herself, Miss Bingley is not above attempting to "provoke Darcy into disliking her guest." She does this by teasing him mercilessly about his future "supposed marriage" to Elizabeth and making cruel comments about Elizabeth's mother, younger sisters, and aunt and uncle. Miss Bingley really wants Mr. Darcy to deny any affection for Elizabeth; when she fails to elicit this response, her insults intensify.

Caroline is practicing the age-old art of "baiting," which is the act of provoking someone to stir up strife. We see it first in the garden, when Satan visits Eve at the Tree and asks coyly, "Did God *really* say, 'You must not eat from any tree in the garden'?" (Genesis 3:1 NIV, emphasis added). When Eve enters into this conversation with the deceiver, she steps right into the trap Satan laid for her.

Today, Satan is still using the same tricks on us. A master manipulator and a crafty strategist, he will stop at nothing to sabotage our relationship with Jesus. When we struggle in a certain area, he senses our weaknesses and baits his hook accordingly.

The next time Satan begins whispering his half-truths in your ear, turn and *run* into the Savior's arms. Identify the bait for what it is—*lies* and *deceit*—and ask God for His strength to withstand the enemy's schemes.

ॐ

PUT ON THE FULL ARMOR OF GOD SO THAT YOU CAN
TAKE YOUR STAND AGAINST THE DEVIL'S SCHEMES.

Ephesians 6:11 NIV

Justifying Sin

Mrs. Jennings laughed heartily; and Elinor found that in her resolution to know where they had been, she had actually made her own woman enquire of Mr. Willoughby's groom; and that she had by that method been informed that they had gone to Allenham, and spent a considerable time therein walking about the garden and going all over the house.

Elinor could hardly believe this to be true, as it seemed very unlikely that Willoughby should propose, or Marianne consent, to enter the house while Mrs. Smith was in it, with whom Marianne had not the smallest acquaintance.

As soon as they left the dining-room, Elinor enquired of her about it; and great was her surprise when she found that every circumstance related by Mrs. Jennings was perfectly true. Marianne was quite angry with her for doubting it.

"Why should you imagine, Elinor, that we did not go there, or that we did not see the house? Is not it what you have often wished to do yourself?"

"Yes, Marianne, but I would not go while Mrs. Smith was there, and with no other companion than Mr. Willoughby."

"Mr. Willoughby however is the only person who can have a right to shew that house; and as he went in an open carriage, it was impossible to have any other companion. I never spent a pleasanter morning in my life."

"I am afraid," replied Elinor, "that the pleasantness of an employment does not always evince its propriety."

—*Sense and Sensibility*

For all of Marianne's merry, flirtatious, expressive ways, she is making poor choices. Her open adoration of Willoughby leaves no one wondering where her affections lie. In a world that honors decorum and propriety, Marianne is treading dangerous waters.

Furthermore, Elinor worries about Marianne and Willoughby's mutual disregard for the opinions of others—and with good reason. Marianne's senses so control her decisions that her virtue cannot be trusted in matters of the heart.

Her most recent example of poor judgment—visiting Allenham alone with Willoughby—demonstrates impropriety for a young woman of that time. That Marianne is defensive and arrogant when questioned about it by Elinor makes her decision all the more dangerous; she is justifying her actions and adding blatant disregard for decorum to the equation.

Sin of *all* forms can creep into our lives. "As the serpent deceived Eve by his cunning, your thoughts will be led astray from a sincere and pure devotion to Christ" (2 Corinthians 11:3). If we allow it to take up residence in our hearts, we deny ourselves close relationship with Christ. To combat this, run to Him! Choose daily to be sensitive to the Spirit's leading in all that you do, and be quick to listen when He lays conviction upon your heart.

❦

LET US GO RIGHT INTO THE PRESENCE OF GOD WITH SINCERE HEARTS FULLY TRUSTING HIM. FOR OUR GUILTY CONSCIENCES HAVE BEEN SPRINKLED WITH CHRIST'S BLOOD TO MAKE US CLEAN, AND OUR BODIES HAVE BEEN WASHED WITH PURE WATER.

Hebrews 10:22 NLT

Appearing Religious

Mr. Collins was not a sensible man, and the deficiency of nature had been but little assisted by education or society; the greatest part of his life having been spent under the guidance of an illiterate and miserly father; and though he belonged to one of the universities, he had merely kept the necessary terms, without forming at it any useful acquaintance. The subjection in which his father had brought him up had given him originally great humility of manner, but it was now a good deal counteracted by the self-conceit of a weak head, living in retirement, and the consequential feelings of early and unexpected prosperity. A fortunate chance had recommended him to Lady Catherine de Bourgh when the living of Hunsford was vacant; and the respect which he felt for her high rank and his veneration for her as his patroness, mingling with a very good opinion of himself, of his authority as a clergyman, and his rights as a rector, made him altogether a mixture of pride and obsequiousness, self-importance and humility.

Having now a good house and very sufficient income, he intended to marry; and in seeking a reconciliation with the Longbourn family he had a wife in view, as he meant to chuse one of the daughters, if he found them as handsome and amiable as they were represented by common report. This was his plan of amends—of atonement—for inheriting their father's estate; and he thought it an excellent one, full of eligibility and suitableness, and excessively generous and disinterested on his own part.

—*Pride and Prejudice*

For Mr. Collins, the primary job of a rector is to say what he thinks everyone around him wants to hear. He is conceited, consumed by his image, and intent on impressing others—most of all his patroness, the Lady Catherine de Bourgh. But worst of all, he completely lacks the ability or desire to shepherd his congregants toward godliness.

Does this kind of religious hypocrisy sound familiar? It should. Mr. Collins's attitude is nearly identical to that of the New Testament Pharisees, who also adhered to a strict moral code but were mostly concerned with religious performance—both theirs and others'.

It is quite telling that the Greek word used in Luke's gospel for *hypocrisy* was a way to describe an actor's performance in a play. Similarly, religious hypocrites like Mr. Collins and the Pharisees approach their duties as actors approach a script: motivated by a burning need for approval, they are obsessed with *appearing* religious.

This explains why the Pharisees were so dumbfounded by Jesus, who "came to seek and to save the lost" (Luke 19:10). The simplicity—the very *others*-centeredness—of Jesus' message does not fit their standard, and they feel threatened. As with anyone who chooses religion over following Jesus, their obsession with performance lets them avoid their own brokenness. They completely miss the point of close relationship with Christ.

Don't be like Mr. Collins or the Pharisees, who needed people to respect them more than they wanted to please God. Make the test of your heart-decisions be whether *God* approves, regardless of what others might say.

❧

AM I NOW TRYING TO WIN THE APPROVAL OF MEN, OR OF GOD?
OR AM I TRYING TO PLEASE MEN? IF I WERE STILL TRYING TO
PLEASE MEN, I WOULD NOT BE A SERVANT OF CHRIST.

Galatians 1:10 NIV

CODDLING COVETOUSNESS

For the first seven miles Miss Bertram had very little real comfort: her prospect always ended in Mr. Crawford and her sister sitting side by side, full of conversation and merriment; and to see only his expressive profile as he turned with a smile to Julia, or to catch the laugh of the other, was a perpetual source of irritation, which her own sense of propriety could but just smooth over. When Julia looked back, it was with a countenance of delight, and whenever she spoke to them, it was in the highest spirits: "her view of the country was charming, she wished they could all see it," etc.; but her only offer of exchange was addressed to Miss Crawford, as they gained the summit of a long hill, and was not more inviting than this: "Here is a fine burst of country. I wish you had my seat, but I dare say you will not take it, let me press you ever so much;" and Miss Crawford could hardly answer before they were moving again at a good pace.

When they came within the influence of Sotherton associations, it was better for Miss Bertram, who might be said to have two strings to her bow. She had Rushworth feelings, and Crawford feelings, and in the vicinity of Sotherton the former had considerable effect. Mr. Rushworth's consequence was hers.

—Mansfield Park

Maria Bertram is a woman at odds with herself. On the one hand, she will soon be Lady Rushworth and able to claim Sotherton estate as her own, a fact that makes her swell with pride; on the other, she is burning up with jealousy over the attention being paid by

Mr. Crawford toward her sister, Julia. Maria is fighting an inner battle with covetousness—and losing badly.

Loosely defined, covetousness is discontent with what we have and a craving for more—in Maria's case, more attention, more wealth, more status. From a biblical perspective, it is a form of idolatry because it promotes jealousy and illicit desire, it wishes ill circumstances on others, and when indulged, it gratifies only temporarily.

Jesus warned His disciples strongly against coveting: "Be on your guard against all covetousness, for one's life does not consist in the abundance of his possessions" (Luke 12:15). It is a slippery slope between coveting what we don't have and taking it for ourselves through illicit means. Developing a covetous spirit does not happen overnight. Maria, a young woman accustomed to getting her way throughout her lifetime, has been schooled to believe that she *deserves* whatever her heart desires. Because of this, she has no safeguards to protect her character or urge her to choose the high road.

Do you covet whatever is lacking in your own life? Do you spend more time dwelling on what you don't have rather than having a grateful heart for what you do have? If so, you'll never be satisfied. Only God can provide true joy and fulfillment here on earth, and only a singular pursuit of Him can ensure it.

⚬❦⚬

"BUT ABOVE ALL PURSUE HIS KINGDOM AND
RIGHTEOUSNESS, AND ALL THESE THINGS WILL BE
GIVEN TO YOU AS WELL."

Matthew 6:33 NET

LETTING GO OF WORRY

Mr. Knightley and Emma settled it in a few brief sentences: thus—"Your father will not be easy; why do not you go?"

"I am ready, if the others are."

"Shall I ring the bell?"

"Yes, do."

And the bell was rung, and the carriages spoken for. A few minutes more, and Emma hoped to see one troublesome companion deposited in his own house, to get sober and cool, and the other recover his temper and happiness when this visit of hardship were over. The carriage came: and Mr. Woodhouse, always the first object on such occasions, was carefully attended to his own by Mr. Knightley and Mr. Weston; but not all that either could say could prevent some renewal of alarm at the sight of the snow which had actually fallen, and the discovery of a much darker night than he had been prepared for. "He was afraid they should have a very bad drive. He was afraid poor Isabella would not like it. And there would be poor Emma in the carriage behind. He did not know what they had best do. They must keep as much together as they could;" and James was talked to, and given a charge to go very slow and wait for the other carriage.

—Emma

It is a fact that if Mr. Woodhouse had nothing to worry about, he would not know what to do with himself. Here we see a dinner party cut short because snow has begun to fall—and in eighteenth-century England, particularly for a hypochondriac like Mr. Woodhouse, that spells one thing: trouble. So home they go, bundled snugly into carriages and conveyed by experienced horsemen. Not that this allays Mr. Woodhouse's concerns! "Poor Emma!" "Poor Isabella!"

While lightly made fun of in this scene, we all understand that worry can be a very real stumbling block. For one, it is a waste of precious time. Arguably, a character like Mr. Woodhouse has ample time to spend worrying—he is a rich landowner with a staff of servants and a doting daughter! But for the vast majority of us, worry does nothing but deplete our energy and steal moments that we can never recover or reclaim.

A second—and equally important—consideration is that time spent worrying is time *not* spent trusting God. That energy would be so much better put to prayer! The Bible tells us, "Don't worry about anything; instead, pray about everything" (Philippians 4:6 NLT).

The next time you are burdened by worry, choose to give your anxious thoughts to God; let Him carry that burden. It is His job, and He wants only to be asked.

❧

"CAN ALL YOUR WORRIES ADD A SINGLE MOMENT TO
YOUR LIFE? AND WHY WORRY ABOUT YOUR CLOTHING?
LOOK AT THE LILIES OF THE FIELD AND HOW THEY
GROW. THEY DON'T WORK OR MAKE THEIR CLOTHING,
YET SOLOMON IN ALL HIS GLORY WAS NOT DRESSED AS
BEAUTIFULLY AS THEY ARE."

Matthew 6:27–29 NLT

Unhealthy Persuasion

[Catherine:] "Do not urge me, Isabella. I am engaged to Miss Tilney. I cannot go." This availed nothing. *The same arguments assailed her again; she must go, she should go, and they would not hear of a refusal. "It would be so easy to tell Miss Tilney that you had just been reminded of a prior engagement, and must only beg to put off the walk till Tuesday."*

"No, it would not be easy. I could not do it. There has been no prior engagement." But Isabella became only more and more urgent, calling on her in the most affectionate manner, addressing her by the most endearing names. She was sure her dearest, sweetest Catherine would not seriously refuse such a trifling request to a friend who loved her so dearly. She knew her beloved Catherine to have so feeling a heart, so sweet a temper, to be so easily persuaded by those she loved. But all in vain; Catherine felt herself to be in the right, and though pained by such tender, such flattering supplication, could not allow it to influence her. Isabella then tried another method. She reproached her with having more affection for Miss Tilney, though she had known her so little a while, than for her best and oldest friends, with being grown cold and indifferent, in short, towards herself. *"I cannot help being jealous, Catherine, when I see myself slighted for strangers, I, who love you so excessively!"*

—*Northanger Abbey*

The closer we are to our friends, the more likely we are to be influenced by them. This proves problematic for girls like Catherine, whose gullibility makes her the perfect target for manipulation. Of all the lessons Catherine will learn in *Northanger Abbey*, one of the most eye-opening is that Isabella cares about no one but herself; she is simply using Catherine for a fun time and a listening ear.

We see Isabella's true colors beginning to come out in the way she teases and pleads and finally demands that Catherine break a promise to go walking with another friend, Miss Tilney. In a final effort to regain Catherine's full attention for herself, Isabella pouts, "I cannot help being jealous, Catherine, when I see myself slighted for strangers, I, who love you so excessively!"

The Bible warns us against spending time with people like Isabella: "Do not be misled: 'Bad company corrupts good character'" (1 Corinthians 15:33 NIV). For Isabella, Catherine exists as nothing more than a plaything, a shoulder to cry on, and a way to flirt with Catherine's brother. Isabella *calls* Catherine her dearest friend, but only when jealous, reproaching her for keeping a promise to spend time with Eleanor. In short, Isabella is a far cry from the example of godly womanhood that God wants us to choose in friendship.

Your closest friendships bear strong witness to how you prioritize God in your life. Seek to develop friendships in which you point each other to Jesus.

ॐ

TWO ARE BETTER THAN ONE, BECAUSE THEY HAVE A
GOOD RETURN FOR THEIR WORK: IF ONE FALLS DOWN,
HIS FRIEND CAN HELP HIM UP.

Ecclesiastes 4:9–10 NIV

Trap of Comparison

Deeply was [Lizzy] vexed to find that her mother was talking to that one person (Lady Lucas) freely, openly, and of nothing else but of her expectation that Jane would be soon married to Mr. Bingley.—It was an animating subject, and Mrs. Bennet seemed incapable of fatigue while enumerating the advantages of the match. His being such a charming young man, and so rich, and living but three miles from them, were the first points of self-gratulation; and then it was such a comfort to think how fond the two sisters were of Jane, and to be certain that they must desire the connection as much as she could do. It was, moreover, such a promising thing for her younger daughters, as Jane's marrying so greatly must throw them in the way of other rich men; and lastly, it was so pleasant at her time of life to be able to consign her single daughters to the care of their sister, that she might not be obliged to go into company more than she liked. It was necessary to make this circumstance a matter of pleasure, because on such occasions it is the etiquette, but no one was less likely than Mrs. Bennet to find comfort in staying at home at any period of her life. She concluded with many good wishes that Lady Lucas might soon be equally fortunate, though evidently and triumphantly believing there was no chance of it.

—Pride and Prejudice

Mrs. Bennet is boasting to Lady Lucas about "her expectation that Jane would be soon married to Mr. Bingley" and the ensuing wealth and opportunity that will doubtless follow for the rest of the Bennet family. She concludes with the ultimate snub: her "good wishes" that Lady Lucas's daughters might be equally fortunate in love and marriage, an obviously hollow form of lip service.

Trying to outdo Mrs. Lucas is what we've come to expect from Mrs. Bennet. But as exaggerated as her character's bravado may be, it reflects a very real predisposition that we all struggle with: trying to make ourselves look and seem better than others.

The antithesis of this can be seen in Moses, the Hebrew prophet who was used mightily of God to lead the Israelite nation out of slavery in Egypt. Despite his high rank, Moses was described this way in Numbers 12: "Now the man Moses was very humble, more than all men who were on the face of the earth" (v. 3 NKJV). Moses understood that leading in humility requires great inner strength.

Do you find yourself stuck in the cycle of comparing yourself to others? Do you secretly long for the smallest waistline, the largest bank account, the best-behaved children, or the next job promotion? You may think this kind of competition makes you stronger, but in God's economy it is a sign of weakness. Ask God to eradicate this tendency and to replace it with genuine acceptance of who you are and contentment with what you have.

❧

THEREFORE, AS THE ELECT OF GOD, HOLY AND
BELOVED, PUT ON TENDER MERCIES, KINDNESS,
HUMILITY, MEEKNESS, LONGSUFFERING.

Colossians 3:12 NKJV

SETTING EMOTIONAL BOUNDARIES

They saw nothing of Marianne till dinner time, when she entered the room and took her place at the table without saying a word. Her eyes were red and swollen; and it seemed as if her tears were even then restrained with difficulty. She avoided the looks of them all, could neither eat nor speak, and after some time, on her mother's silently pressing her hand with tender compassion, her small degree of fortitude was quite overcome, she burst into tears and left the room.

This violent oppression of spirits continued the whole evening. She was without any power, because she was without any desire of command over herself. The slightest mention of anything relative to Willoughby overpowered her in an instant; and though her family were most anxiously attentive to her comfort, it was impossible for them, if they spoke at all, to keep clear of every subject which her feelings connected with him.

Marianne would have thought herself very inexcusable had she been able to sleep at all the first night after parting from Willoughby. She would have been ashamed to look her family in the face the next morning, had she not risen from her bed in more need of repose than when she lay down in it. But the feelings which made such composure a disgrace, left her in no danger of incurring it. She was awake the whole night, and she wept the greatest part of it. She got up with a headache, was unable to talk, and unwilling to take any nourishment; giving pain every moment to her mother and sisters, and forbidding all attempt at consolation from either. Her sensibility was potent enough!

—Sense and Sensibility

Marianne is indulging in a good, old-fashioned pity party. Of course, to her sensory-driven mind frame, it is *much* more bleak than that: her heart is *wretchedly* bruised by Willoughby's departure. In this scene, one sentence in particular tells us everything about Marianne: "She was without any power, *because she was without any desire of command over herself*" (emphasis added). Marianne has set no emotional boundaries in her life—even if such an idea occurred to her, she would scorn it as repressive.

Herein lies the great difference between the sisters. Where Elinor's careful attention to her emotions and interactions creates remarkable self-possession, Marianne's all-too-free emotional expression grows into self-absorption. One goes through life with cautious sensibility; the other is drawn to its fullest expression of the senses. Each approach has both benefits and drawbacks. However, in this scene we see Marianne's clear need for emotional boundaries, particularly in the area of her emotions.

But where do we begin in setting appropriate boundaries? By going to God, who "teaches us to say 'No' to ungodliness and worldly passions, and to live self-controlled, upright and godly lives in this present age" (Titus 2:12 NIV). Unlike putting up walls, boundaries are intended to protect us so that we can grow stronger in the Lord.

◦◦

BE SELF-CONTROLLED IN ALL THINGS.

2 Timothy 4:5 NET

A Disciplined Prayer Life

Mrs. Rushworth began her relation. "This chapel was fitted up as you see it, in James the Second's time. Before that period, as I understand, the pews were only wainscot; and there is some reason to think that the linings and cushions of the pulpit and family seat were only purple cloth; but this is not quite certain. It is a handsome chapel, and was formerly in constant use both morning and evening. Prayers were always read in it by the domestic chaplain, within the memory of many; but the late Mr. Rushworth left it off."

"Every generation has its improvements," said Miss Crawford, with a smile, to Edmund. . . .

"It is a pity," cried Fanny, "that the custom should have been discontinued. It was a valuable part of former times. There is something in a chapel and chaplain so much in character with a great house, with one's ideas of what such a household should be! A whole family assembling regularly for the purpose of prayer is fine!"

"Very fine indeed," said Miss Crawford, laughing. "It must do the heads of the family a great deal of good to force all the poor housemaids and footmen to leave business and pleasure, and say their prayers here twice a day, while they are inventing excuses themselves for staying away."

"That is hardly Fanny's idea of a family assembling," said Edmund. "If the master and mistress do not attend themselves, there must be more harm than good in the custom."

—*Mansfield Park*

U naware that Edmund intends to take orders to become a clergyman, Miss Crawford laughingly offers the opinion that the cessation of regular prayer services at Sotherton chapel is an "improvement." This irreverent view on corporate prayer contrasts starkly with Fanny's warm opinion: "A whole family assembling regularly for the purpose of prayer is fine!"

Fanny is an advocate of family, home, and church activity, and she sees clear benefits to formal religious gatherings; by contrast, Mary Crawford is a big-city girl who finds chapel services boring, obligatory, and unnecessary. Their opposing viewpoints reveal much about the heart of each woman's character, in no small part because regular prayer time requires something wholly lacking in Mary's life. devotion.

The value of time spent praying cannot be overestimated. Regular prayer was an example first set by Jesus, who throughout His ministry would "withdraw to desolate places and pray" (Luke 5:16). In turn, Jesus' apostles followed suit—and as Christ followers, we are encouraged to do the same. The many benefits to prayer include communing with God, learning to listen for His voice, and letting His words and thoughts guide our lives. Think of that! *We have a direct means of communicating with God.* When we pray, we speak the language of our relationship with Him.

If you desire to be a true disciple of Christ—if you want to become like Him—there is no better place to start than with consistent, devoted prayer.

୧ৡৢ৩

NOW JESUS WAS PRAYING IN A CERTAIN PLACE, AND
WHEN HE FINISHED, ONE OF HIS DISCIPLES SAID TO
HIM, "LORD, TEACH US TO PRAY."

Luke 11:1

Danger of Self-Importance

Perhaps it was not fair to expect [Mr. Elton] to feel how very much he was her inferior in talent, and all the elegancies of mind. The very want of such equality might prevent his perception of it; but he must know that in fortune and consequence she was greatly his superior. He must know that the Woodhouses had been settled for several generations at Hartfield, the younger branch of a very ancient family—and that the Eltons were nobody. The landed property of Hartfield certainly was inconsiderable, being but a sort of notch in the Donwell Abbey estate, to which all the rest of Highbury belonged; but their fortune, from other sources, was such as to make them scarcely secondary to Donwell Abbey itself, in every other kind of consequence; and the Woodhouses had long held a high place in the consideration of the neighbourhood which Mr. Elton had first entered not two years ago, to make his way as he could, without any alliances but in trade, or any thing to recommend him to notice but his situation and his civility.—But he had fancied her in love with him; that evidently must have been his dependence; and after raving a little about the seeming incongruity of gentle manners and a conceited head, Emma was obliged in common honesty to stop and admit that her own behaviour to him had been so complaisant and obliging, so full of courtesy and attention, as (supposing her real motive unperceived) might warrant a man of ordinary observation and delicacy, like Mr. Elton, in fancying himself a very decided favourite. If she had so misinterpreted his feelings, she had little right to wonder that he, with self-interest to blind him, should have mistaken hers.

—Emma

In this comical scene, Emma lists her enormous fortune as a reason she is superior to Mr. Elton. Her mental cataloging does not stop at her vast financial resources, however—she also considers him "her inferior in talent, and all the elegancies of mind."

Emma has long promoted a match between Mr. Elton and her dear friend Harriet, an idea scorned roundly by Mr. Elton; yet when Mr. Elton professes affection for Emma, he is derided for daring to imagine her his equal. Emma is so insulted by Mr. Elton's blinding self-interest that she cannot see how her own object (making a match between Harriet and Mr. Elton) blinds her as well!

When our pride is threatened, it is easy to grow defensive and act superior, like Emma. Sure, we might *say* that we honor Jesus' second greatest command, "Love your neighbor as yourself" (Matthew 22:39 NIV); but if our hackles rise when someone oversteps a boundary—as Mr. Elton's did with Emma—it is a clear indication that we need to reevaluate whether we have love or self-interest as our priority. Emma's heart issue is not that she refused Mr. Elton—it was the correct thing to do, considering the circumstances. Rather, it is her failure to treat him with love but instead, blistering scorn.

As Christians, we are to honor Jesus' command to "love your neighbor" by extending kindness to *all* people, regardless of social standing, education, ethnicity, or vocation. In fact, we are to go even a step further by "in humility considering others better than yourselves" (Philippians 2:3 NIV).

৵

"You shall love the Lord your God with all your heart and with all your soul and with all your mind. This is the great and first commandment. And a second is like it: You shall love your neighbor as yourself."

Matthew 22:37–39

To Elizabeth it appeared, that had her family made an agreement to expose themselves as much as they could during the evening, it would have been impossible for them to play their parts with more spirit, or finer success; and happy did she think it for Bingley and her sister that some of the exhibition had escaped his notice, and that his feelings were not of a sort to be much distressed by the folly which he must have witnessed. That his two sisters and Mr. Darcy, however, should have such an opportunity of ridiculing her relations was bad enough, and she could not determine whether the silent contempt of the gentleman, or the insolent smiles of the ladies, were more intolerable.

The rest of the evening brought her little amusement. She was teazed by Mr. Collins, who continued most perseveringly by her side, and though he could not prevail with her to dance with him again, put it out of her power to dance with others. In vain did she entreat him to stand up with somebody else, and offer to introduce him to any young lady in the room. He assured her that as to dancing, he was perfectly indifferent to it; that his chief object was by delicate attentions to recommend himself to her, and that he should therefore make a point of remaining close to her the whole evening. There was no arguing upon such a project.

—*Pride and Prejudice*

If it were possibly to replace one's family, Elizabeth Bennet would be looking at an almost entirely different cast of characters. She is frequently horrified by things they say and do, both accidental and intentional. Even worse, her mortification is justified: Elizabeth finds out later that

Mr. Darcy has fallen in love with her *in spite of* her family's embarrassing performance.

It is not uncommon to be embarrassed by one's own family. However, as Christians we are commanded to treat one another with respect and dignity, whether or not we wish—like Elizabeth—that we could run away and hide.

The way we respond in humiliating moments reveals a lot about our character. Take, for example, Joseph, the father of Jesus. In Matthew 1, Joseph is described as "a just man" (v. 19) who finds out that his fiancée, Mary, is pregnant. Joseph has every right to feel disgraced because he knows the child isn't his. His first reaction—to break off the engagement between them—is done with great kindness and compassion for Mary. And after an angel visits Joseph and verifies Mary's story, Joseph willingly obeys God and reinstates the engagement.

Joseph does all this despite the public humiliation he knows he will face. As both a father and a husband, Joseph demonstrates integrity and righteousness in the face of likely shame and disgrace. Perhaps this is why God chose Joseph—so that we might see how an honorable man treats his family respectfully despite the public's perception of oddity or dishonor.

The next time you cringe when a certain relative opens her mouth to speak, look at the character of the man God chose to be the Messiah's earthly father. Then consider swallowing your pride and choosing kindness over judgment.

‹❧›

SO WHY DO YOU CONDEMN ANOTHER BELIEVER?
WHY DO YOU LOOK DOWN ON ANOTHER BELIEVER?
REMEMBER, WE WILL ALL STAND BEFORE THE
JUDGMENT SEAT OF GOD.

Romans 14:10 NLT

FEELING SORRY FOR ONESELF

Though better endowed than [Elizabeth], Mary had not Anne's under-standing nor temper. While well, and happy, and properly attended to, she had great good humour and excellent spirits; but any indisposition sunk her completely. She had no resources for solitude; and inheriting a considerable share of the Elliot self-importance, was very prone to add to every other distress that of fancying herself neglected and ill-used. In person, she was inferior to both sisters, and had, even in her bloom, only reached the dignity of being "a fine girl." She was now lying on the faded sofa of the pretty little drawing-room, the once elegant furniture of which had been gradually growing shabby, under the influence of four summers and two children; and, on Anne's appearing, greeted her with—

"So, you are come at last! I began to think I should never see you. I am so ill I can hardly speak. I have not seen a creature the whole morning!"

"I am sorry to find you unwell," replied Anne. "You sent me such a good account of yourself on Thursday!"

"Yes, I made the best of it; I always do: but I was very far from well at the time; and I do not think I ever was so ill in my life as I have been all this morning: very unfit to be left alone, I am sure. Suppose I were to be seized of a sudden in some dreadful way, and not able to ring the bell!"

—Persuasion

The youngest Elliot sister, Mary, is a confirmed hypochondriac whose suffering stems from one source: she has inherited "a considerable share of the Elliot *self-importance.*" Mary's belief that she is always ill or even dying from her aches and pains is quickly revealed as her favorite way of getting attention; when her suffering does not elicit the desired level of sympathy, she assumes an air of martyrdom.

Like Mary, many Christians live in a heightened state of hypochondria— only ours is of a spiritual nature. So many of us do not know how to be happy with what we've been given; it's much easier to focus on being miserable!

This is exactly how the children of Israel acted after they were rescued from slavery in Egypt, brought through the Red Sea, and given food and drink from heaven. Look at their response: "Again the Israelites started wailing and said, 'If only we had meat to eat! We remember the fish we ate in Egypt at no cost—also the cucumbers, melons, leeks, onions and garlic. But now we have lost our appetite; we never see anything but this manna!'" (Numbers 11:4–6 NIV). With every new blessing came a new grievance. How quickly they forgot that they had been rescued from four hundred years of slavery!

If you're like Mary, you sometimes find yourself consumed by your lot—perhaps even wallowing in unhappiness. Take a good look at your circumstance and see if you are simply behaving like the children of Israel: ignoring God's blessings in your life and making it all about you.

❧

CONSIDER IT ALL JOY, MY BRETHREN, WHEN YOU
ENCOUNTER VARIOUS TRIALS, KNOWING THAT THE
TESTING OF YOUR FAITH PRODUCES ENDURANCE. AND LET
ENDURANCE HAVE ITS PERFECT RESULT, SO THAT YOU MAY
BE PERFECT AND COMPLETE, LACKING IN NOTHING.

James 1:2–4 NASB

SELF-DECEPTION

*[Mr. Collins to Elizabeth, following his proposal:] "You must give me leave
to flatter myself, my dear cousin, that your refusal of my addresses is merely
words of course. My reasons for believing it are briefly these:—It does not
appear to me that my hand is unworthy your acceptance, or that the estab-
lishment I can offer would be any other than highly desirable. My situation
in life, my connections with the family of De Bourgh, and my relationship to
your own, are circumstances highly in its favor; and you should take it into
farther consideration that in spite of your manifold attractions, it is by no
means certain that another offer of marriage may ever be made you. Your
portion is unhappily so small that it will in all likelihood undo the effects of
your loveliness and amiable qualifications.". . . .*

*"I do assure you, Sir, that I have no pretension whatever to that kind of
elegance which consists in tormenting a respectable man. I would rather be
paid the compliment of being believed sincere. I thank you again and again
for the honour you have done me in your proposals, but to accept them is
absolutely impossible. My feelings in every respect forbid it. Can I speak
plainer? Do not consider me now as an elegant female intending to plague
you, but as a rational creature speaking the truth from her heart."*

*"You are uniformly charming!" cried he, with an air of awkward gal-
lantry; "and I am persuaded that when sanctioned by the express authority of
both your excellent parents, my proposals will not fail of being acceptable."*

*To such perseverance in wilful self-deception, Elizabeth would make
no reply.*

—Pride and Prejudice

Finally Mr. Collins has proposed, and Elizabeth is doing her best to turn him down. But a man as pompous as Mr. Collins is difficult to dissuade, especially in a circumstance like this—where he considers himself the more esteemed party. Elizabeth's protests fall on deaf ears as Collins reiterates, comedically, the many reasons she could not *possibly* be saying no.

Mr. Collins, for reasons unknown, is bent on getting through life *not* seeing things as they truly are—neither his spiritual duties as rector, nor his community standing, nor even his own emotions regarding love and marriage. His obsequious behavior toward Lady Catherine de Bourgh is evidence that he craves recognition and status. His inability to comprehend Elizabeth's refusal aligns perfectly with his own puffed-up perception of himself.

The Bible warns against this type of willful self-deception in 1 Corinthians: "Let no man deceive himself. If any man among you thinks that he is wise in this age, he must become foolish, so that he may become wise" (3:18 NASB). In other words, we have to become willing to be "foolish" for Christ—to trust Him even when the circumstances don't make sense.

What we practice—what we truly believe—is indicative of what's in our hearts. Deceiving ourselves is the same thing as believing we know better than God. Our relationship with Him cannot thrive if we fail to let Him inside our hearts to purify them.

❧

FINALLY, BROTHERS, WHATEVER IS TRUE, WHATEVER IS
HONORABLE, WHATEVER IS JUST, WHATEVER IS PURE,
WHATEVER IS LOVELY, WHATEVER IS COMMENDABLE,
IF THERE IS ANY EXCELLENCE, IF THERE IS ANYTHING
WORTHY OF PRAISE, THINK ABOUT THESE THINGS.

Philippians 4:8

In Support of Clergy

Miss Crawford began with, "So you are to be a clergyman, Mr. Bertram. This is rather a surprise to me."

"Why should it surprise you? You must suppose me designed for some profession, and might perceive that I am neither a lawyer, nor a soldier, nor a sailor."

"Very true; but, in short, it had not occurred to me. And you know there is generally an uncle or a grandfather to leave a fortune to the second son."

"A very praiseworthy practice," said Edmund, "but not quite universal. I am one of the exceptions, and being one, must do something for myself."

"But why are you to be a clergyman? I thought that was always the lot of the youngest, where there were many to chuse before him."

"Do you think the church itself never chosen, then?"

"Never is a black word. But yes, in the never of conversation, which means not very often, I do think it. For what is to be done in the church? Men love to distinguish themselves, and in either of the other lines distinction may be gained, but not in the church. A clergyman is nothing."

—*Mansfield Park*

In the course of this short conversation, it becomes increasingly clear that Mary Crawford has no respect for the clergy. The motive behind her disregard is twofold: a lack of religious upbringing, and a desire to marry a wealthy gentleman (because Edmund has caught her eye, she is determined that he will aspire to a level of importance that suits her).

According to Mary's logic, a man lacks any opportunity to "distinguish" himself as a pastor; she goes so far as to declare, "A clergyman is nothing." What Mary doesn't seem to realize is that her irreverence toward the pastoral office is demeaning to Edmund, both professionally and personally.

This flagrant irreverence must make the observing Fanny wonder: what clergyman would want to be married to Mary Crawford? Certainly we are wondering the same, especially when we see in Scripture the importance of showing reverence to pastors: "The elders who rule well are to be considered worthy of double honor, especially those who work hard at preaching and teaching" (1 Timothy 5:17 NASB). That Edmund cannot see Mary's disrespect is evidence that he is duped by her wiles—ironically, that he lacks the very judgment he will need in his role as clergyman.

By biblical standards, reverencing a pastor means honoring him with your words, actions, and thoughts; encouraging, praying for, and building him up. But most important, it entails something for which Mary Crawford seems to care not: a pastor is an important advocate, a shepherd who helps guide us in our walk with Christ.

❧

THE MASTER DIRECTED THAT THOSE WHO SPREAD
THE MESSAGE BE SUPPORTED BY THOSE WHO
BELIEVE THE MESSAGE.

1 Corinthians 9:14 MSG

APPRECIATING YOUR SPOUSE

Charlotte laughed heartily to think that her husband could not get rid of her; and exultingly said, she did not care how cross he was to her, as they must live together.

It was impossible for any one to be more thoroughly good-natured, or more determined to be happy than Mrs. Palmer.

The studied indifference, insolence, and discontent of her husband gave her no pain; and when he scolded or abused her, she was highly diverted.

"Mr. Palmer is so droll!" said she, in a whisper, to Elinor. "He is always out of humour."

Elinor was not inclined, after a little observation, to give him credit for being so genuinely and unaffectedly ill-natured or ill-bred as he wished to appear. His temper might perhaps be a little soured by finding, like many others of his sex, that through some unaccountable bias in favour of beauty, he was the husband of a very silly woman,—but she knew that this kind of blunder was too common for any sensible man to be lastingly hurt by it.—It was rather a wish of distinction, she believed, which produced his contemptuous treatment of every body, and his general abuse of every thing before him.

It was the desire of appearing superior to other people. The motive was too common to be wondered at; but the means, however they might succeed by establishing his superiority in ill-breeding, were not likely to attach any one to him except his wife.

—Sense and Sensibility

Mr. Palmer, as Elinor observes, "through some un- accountable bias in favour of beauty . . . was the husband of a very silly woman." His wife might well be good-natured, quick to laugh, and determined to be happy—but she is nearly *unbearably* silly, a fact that goads Mr. Palmer at every turn.

Readers are quick to note that Mr. Palmer's ill tem- per hardly renders him a prize husband. The superiority he asserts over his wife is constant and inexcusably rude. Oddly, Mrs. Palmer's grand political aspirations for her hus- band (he *will* be prime minister, if she has her way) blind her to his faults: he is only "droll," never bad mannered or ill-tempered. Neither has a clear picture of the other.

Perhaps this is because in Jane Austen's culture, marry- ing well could ensure material comfort for a lifetime; whether it meant marital happiness was nearly beside the point. It is this fact that causes Elinor to marvel at "the strange un- suitableness which often existed between husband and wife."

As Christians, we know it was not intended to be so. Marriage is sacred before God, and romantic love is a gift ordained by Him. Furthermore, it is a picture given by God to reflect His Son's devotion to the church—a willingness to lay down His life for her.

The benefits to showing honor and respect toward the one you love and to whom you commit your life are many. Think about your marriage. Do you appreciate your spouse as a God-given gift? Do you treat him with the honor accorded by the sanctity of marriage?

❦

LET HIM KISS ME WITH THE KISSES OF HIS MOUTH—
FOR YOUR LOVE IS MORE DELIGHTFUL THAN WINE.

Song of Solomon 1:2 NIV

REST AND REFRESHMENT

[Emma] stopt to blush and laugh at her own relapse, and then resumed a more serious, more dispiriting cogitation upon what had been, and might be, and must be. The distressing explanation she had to make to Harriet, and all that poor Harriet would be suffering, with the awkwardness of future meetings, the difficulties of continuing or discontinuing the acquaintance, of subduing feelings, concealing resentment, and avoiding eclat, were enough to occupy her in most unmirthful reflections some time longer, and she went to bed at last with nothing settled but the conviction of her having blundered most dreadfully.

To youth and natural cheerfulness like Emma's, though under temporary gloom at night, the return of day will hardly fail to bring return of spirits. The youth and cheerfulness of morning are in happy analogy, and of powerful operation; and if the distress be not poignant enough to keep the eyes unclosed, they will be sure to open to sensations of softened pain and brighter hope.

Emma got up on the morrow more disposed for comfort than she had gone to bed, more ready to see alleviations of the evil before her, and to depend on getting tolerably out of it.

—Emma

Sometimes, nothing ushers in a fresh perspective like a good night's sleep. This is certainly true for Emma, whose "youthfulness is aligned with natural cheerfulness." Despite the previous night's guilt over the fiasco she created with Mr. Elton, Emma's heavy conscience is lightened considerably by the dawn of a new morning.

Emma would no doubt agree that sleep is one of God's great gifts to all His creatures. Among its many benefits, sleep lets our bodies rebuild and our thoughts be renewed. Our need for sleep is also a reflection of being made in God's image: He set the example by resting on the seventh day of Creation.

But resting is about more than nourishing body and soul; it is also a picture of surrender. When we seek our refreshment in Him, we choose to follow His path for our lives, we lean into Him, and we accept His gifts of forgiveness, guidance, and sustenance.

In Psalm 4:1, David begged, "Answer me when I call, O God of my righteousness!" Yet just seven verses later he wrote, "In peace I will both lie down and sleep; for you alone, O LORD, make me dwell in safety" (Psalm 4:8). He went from pleading, to dismayed, to self-commanding, finally to relinquishment—and then to sleep.

Psalm 4 offers a full picture of the surrendered life: despite life-threatening dangers all around, David chose God's peace and acknowledged His sovereignty. Through his example, we are reminded that no matter what our circumstances, we can sleep peacefully when we put our trust in the Lord.

Make the decision today to lie down in peace, to trust in God alone, and to accept His gift of rest.

᭟

JOY COMES WITH THE MORNING.

Psalm 30.5

"I see what you are feeling," replied Charlotte,—"you must be surprised, very much surprised,—so lately as Mr. Collins was wishing to marry you. But when you have had time to think it all over, I hope you will be satisfied with what I have done. I am not romantic, you know. I never was. I ask only a comfortable home; and considering Mr. Collins's character, connections, and situation in life, I am convinced that my chance of happiness with him is as fair as most people can boast on entering the marriage state."

Elizabeth quietly answered "Undoubtedly;"—and after an awkward pause, they returned to the rest of the family. Charlotte did not stay much longer, and Elizabeth was then left to reflect on what she had heard. It was a long time before she became at all reconciled to the idea of so unsuitable a match. The strangeness of Mr. Collins's making two offers of marriage within three days, was nothing in comparison of his being now accepted. She had always felt that Charlotte's opinion of matrimony was not exactly like her own, but she could not have supposed it possible that, when called into action, she would have sacrificed every better feeling to worldly advantage. Charlotte the wife of Mr. Collins, was a most humiliating picture!—And to the pang of a friend disgracing herself and sunk in her esteem, was added the distressing conviction that it was impossible for that friend to be tolerably happy in the lot she had chosen.

—Pride and Prejudice

ot three days have passed since Mr. Collins proposed to Elizabeth, yet he has already transferred his affections to Charlotte Lucas—who has inexplicably accepted his marriage proposal. Elizabeth is, understandably, astounded; she questions whether she even *knows* her friend Charlotte, who in accepting Mr. Collins has "sacrificed every better feeling to worldly advantage." It is nearly incomprehensible to Elizabeth's romantic sensitivity that a woman could marry without love.

The situation is reminiscent of the biblical story of Leah, first wife of the Hebrew patriarch Jacob. Plain, older sister Leah was the least favored of Jacob's two wives—due to the fact that he was deceived by her father, Laban, into marrying Leah after working seven years for her younger sister, Rachel. "When morning came, there was Leah! So Jacob said to Laban, 'What is this you have done to me? I served you for Rachel, didn't I? Why have you deceived me?'" (Genesis 29:25 NIV).

For Leah, this must have been excruciating. Imagine knowing that your husband not only doesn't want to be married to *you*, but that your father has tricked him and that he desires your sister instead. How would you even function as a wife? Could you trust that God's will is to accept your circumstances? We have the benefit of seeing God's purpose for Leah's marriage: it is through the direct lineage of Leah and Jacob's son, Judah, that Jesus Christ is born.

Do you feel as if life has handed you unfair circumstances while it seems as though everyone else is being blessed? Do you believe that looking for the best in your circumstances, like Charlotte Lucas, is the outlook God wants you to have? God always has a plan, even when we don't recognize or understand it. Whatever your lot, remember this—because you play a major role in it.

⋘⋙

FOR IT IS GOD WHO WORKS IN YOU TO WILL AND TO
ACT ACCORDING TO HIS GOOD PURPOSE.

Philippians 2:13 NIV

ON DOING RIGHT

Away walked Catherine in great agitation, as fast as the crowd would permit her, fearful of being pursued, yet determined to persevere. As she walked, she reflected on what had passed. It was painful to her to disappoint and displease them, particularly to displease her brother; but she could not repent her resistance. Setting her own inclination apart, to have failed a second time in her engagement to Miss Tilney, to have retracted a promise voluntarily made only five minutes before, and on a false pretence too, must have been wrong. She had not been withstanding them on selfish principles alone, she had not consulted merely her own gratification; that might have been ensured in some degree by the excursion itself, by seeing Blaize Castle; no, she had attended to what was due to others, and to her own character in their opinion. Her conviction of being right, however, was not enough to restore her composure; till she had spoken to Miss Tilney she could not be at ease; and quickening her pace when she got clear of the Crescent, she almost ran over the remaining ground till she gained the top of Milsom Street. . . .

"I am come in a great hurry—It was all a mistake—I never promised to go—I told them from the first I could not go.—I ran away in a great hurry to explain it.—I did not care what you thought of me.—I would not stay for the servant."

—*Northanger Abbey*

Catherine's jumbled thoughts indicate inner turmoil: she is working to understand her confused heart, to decipher her motives for turning her back on one friend to pursue another. It is a clear indication of the undeveloped sense of right and wrong that Catherine is struggling to come to terms with. Ultimately, she weighs the principle of the matter against her own feelings—her wants and desires—and is able to enjoy the comforting conviction that she was correct to resist Isabella's entreaties (though it pained her to disappoint her friend) and to pursue right relationship with Miss Tilney.

For Catherine, who prides herself on indulging in vapid romance novels for entertainment, this "seeking and finding" is a big step toward maturity. She is being forced to examine her motives and make a difficult but necessary decision about her choices.

As Christians, we carry a responsibility to examine our own hearts as we seek spiritual maturity. This requires being disciplined about spending time every day with God. King David understood the vital importance of this discipline. Like each of us, David had distractions and responsibilities pulling him in every direction, but he made a vow: "Lord, in the morning you will hear me; in the morning I will present my case to you and then wait expectantly for an answer" (Psalm 5:3 net).

Morning-by-morning steadfastness in our God-time yields great rewards for our spiritual lives: as we seek to know Him more intimately—as we allow Him to shape our decisions and guide our thoughts—we are gradually transformed into the likeness of His Son.

If you desire with all your heart to grow in the Father's will, then press in to Him—daily. Ask Him to search your heart, to help you take the right steps, to make wise choices that honor Him.

⟡

Search me, O God, and know my heart!
Try me and know my thoughts!

Psalm 139:23

FLIRTING WITH SIN

[Henry Crawford:] "And for the world you would not get out without the key and without Mr. Rushworth's authority and protection, or I think you might with little difficulty pass round the edge of the gate, here, with my assistance; I think it might be done, if you really wished to be more at large, and could allow yourself to think it not prohibited."

[Maria Bertram:] "Prohibited! nonsense! I certainly can get out that way, and I will. Mr. Rushworth will be here in a moment, you know; we shall not be out of sight."

"Or if we are, Miss Price will be so good as to tell him that he will find us near that knoll: the grove of oak on the knoll."

Fanny, feeling all this to be wrong, could not help making an effort to prevent it. "You will hurt yourself, Miss Bertram," she cried. "You had better not go."

Her cousin was safe on the other side while these words were spoken, and, smiling with all the good-humour of success, she said, "Thank you, my dear Fanny, but I and my gown are alive and well, and so good-bye."

—*Mansfield Park*

Stolid, eager-to-please Mr. Rushworth has run off to fetch a gate key, and in his absence Maria Bertram and Henry Crawford are entertaining the idea of slipping through the side gate and exploring the woods together . . . alone. Taunting Maria, Henry suggests that as Mr. Rushworth's betrothed, she is caught in his cage—"you would not get out without the key and without Mr. Rushworth's authority and protection." He then adds teasingly, "I think it might be done, if you really wished to be more at large." These words are all Maria needs to hear. She has been flirting with trouble since she met Henry, and she is more than willing to dance away with him beyond Mr. Rushworth's reach.

Like Maria, we so often vacillate between faithful devotion to God and love of the world and its allure. Every time we choose to taste the forbidden fruit, we are effectively choosing sin over Him. We think we can play around with sin but not get burned; when we do that, we buy into the lie of self-deception.

It is the same lie that the children of Israel believed when Moses went up to the mountain to visit God. In Moses' absence, the Israelites began to question whether he would return. Eventually they begged Aaron, "Make us gods who shall go before us. As for this Moses, . . . we do not know what has become of him" (Exodus 32:1). In the short time that Moses was gone, they turned their hearts toward other sinful pleasures and began to worship false gods.

Don't let your heart be deceived or led astray by the Henry Crawfords of this world. What feels fun or enticing in the moment, if it runs contrary to God's will, may carry a lifetime of consequence. Endeavor to maintain the high standard that God has called you to; it carries the reward of the words, "Well done, faithful servant."

෧෴ඉ

DON'T TURN OFF THE ROAD OF GOODNESS;
KEEP AWAY FROM EVIL PATHS.

Proverbs 4:27 NCV

"*I cannot believe it. Why should they try to influence him? They can only wish his happiness, and if he is attached to me, no other woman can secure it.*"

"*Your first position is false. They may wish many things besides his happiness; they may wish his increase of wealth and consequence; they may wish him to marry a girl who has all the importance of money, great connections, and pride.*"

"*Beyond a doubt, they do wish him to chuse Miss Darcy,*" replied Jane; "*but this may be from better feelings than you are supposing. They have known her much longer than they have known me; no wonder if they love her better. But, whatever may be their own wishes, it is very unlikely they should have opposed their brother's. What sister would think herself at liberty to do it, unless there were something very objectionable? If they believed him attached to me, they would not try to part us; if he were so, they could not succeed. By supposing such an affection, you make every body acting unnaturally and wrong, and me most unhappy. Do not distress me by the idea. I am not ashamed of having been mistaken—or, at least, it is slight, it is nothing in comparison of what I should feel in thinking ill of him or his sisters. Let me take it in the best light, in the light in which it may be understood.*"

—Pride and Prejudice

Jane's gentle manner serves as a foil for her sister's fiery, tempestuous spirit, which is on full display in this scene: Elizabeth is trying to convince her that Mr. Bingley's sisters care more about appearances and wealth than friendship and behaving honorably. But Jane insists that the ladies' motives are pure, and accounts for their hurtful actions by assuming herself mistaken about Mr. Bingley's early affection. Jane's speech is laden with humility and hope: "I am not ashamed of having been mistaken. . . . Let me take it in the best light."

In Jane we have a rare example of someone who follows the true biblical definition of love. Humanity's overwhelming tendency is to jump to conclusions, or expect the worst to avoid disappointment, or turn our backs on people who hurt us. Yet the Bible says, "Love never gives up, never loses faith, is always hopeful, and endures through every circumstance" (1 Corinthians 13:7 NLT).

The extent to which we demonstrate this kind of love requires God's operative grace in our lives. It becomes possible by remembering that it's *not about us*; it's about dying to self and surrendering our sinful tendencies to Christ. When we do, we are freed up to love each other as we want to be loved ourselves . . . as we are loved by Christ.

Think about the area of love where you struggle most. Identify it, submit it to Christ, and begin letting His love flow through you to other imperfect humans.

❧

"A NEW COMMANDMENT I GIVE TO YOU, THAT YOU
LOVE ONE ANOTHER: JUST AS I HAVE LOVED YOU,
YOU ALSO ARE TO LOVE ONE ANOTHER."

John 13:34

DISCIPLINING YOUR CHILDREN IN LOVE

A fond mother . . . in pursuit of praise for her children, the most rapacious of human beings, is likewise the most credulous; her demands are exorbitant; but she will swallow any thing; and the excessive affection and endurance of the Miss Steeles towards her offspring were viewed therefore by Lady Middleton without the smallest surprise or distrust. . . .

"John is in such spirits today!" said she, on his taking Miss Steeles's pocket handkerchief, and throwing it out of the window—"He is full of monkey tricks."

And soon afterwards, on the second boy's violently pinching one of the same lady's fingers, she fondly observed, "How playful William is!"

"And here is my sweet little Annamaria," she added, tenderly caressing a little girl of three years old, who had not made a noise for the last two minutes; "And she is always so gentle and quiet—Never was there such a quiet little thing!"

But unfortunately in bestowing these embraces, a pin in her ladyship's head dress slightly scratching the child's neck, produced from this pattern of gentleness such violent screams, as could hardly be outdone by any creature professedly noisy.

The mother's consternation was excessive; but it could not surpass the alarm of the Miss Steeles, and every thing was done by all three, in so critical an emergency, which affection could suggest as likely to assuage the agonies of the little sufferer.

She was seated in her mother's lap, covered with kisses, her wound bathed with lavender-water, by one of the Miss Steeles, who was on her knees to attend her, and her mouth stuffed with sugar plums by the other.

With such a reward for her tears, the child was too wise to cease crying.

—Sense and Sensibility

Though this scene is humorous, we also glimpse the real danger of excessively indulging one's children. The young Middletons' naughty antics are remarked upon approvingly by their haughty mother, and the Miss Steeles share equal blame for praising their poor behavior. It does not take even the wisdom of the quietly observing Dashwood sisters to recognize that wanting character is being formed—through wanting leadership—before their eyes.

The scriptural view on parental discipline is, at its heart, about our own willingness to submit our pride to God: "The Lord disciplines those he loves, and he punishes everyone he accepts as a son" (Hebrews 12:6 NIV). We have the same responsibility to steward our children toward upright living. A correct view on godly discipline is not about raising perfect children; rather, it is about loving them enough to train them in godliness and with an eternal perspective.

When we exemplify godly submission for our children in our own lives, we get to see their attitudes change, little by little. They become a joy to be around, not for their perfect performance, but for the privilege of witnessing their hearts' response to His shepherding.

❧

IF YOU CORRECT YOUR CHILDREN,
THEY WILL BRING YOU PEACE
AND HAPPINESS.

Proverbs 29:17 CEV

Hope in the Lord, Not Man

Mr. Frank Churchill did not come. When the time proposed drew near, Mrs. Weston's fears were justified in the arrival of a letter of excuse. For the present, he could not be spared, to his "very great mortification and regret; but still he looked forward with the hope of coming to Randalls at no distant period."

Mrs. Weston was exceedingly disappointed—much more disappointed, in fact, than her husband, though her dependence on seeing the young man had been so much more sober: but a sanguine temper, though for ever expecting more good than occurs, does not always pay for its hopes by any proportionate depression. It soon flies over the present failure, and begins to hope again. For half an hour Mr. Weston was surprized and sorry; but then he began to perceive that Frank's coming two or three months later would be a much better plan; better time of year; better weather; and that he would be able, without any doubt, to stay considerably longer with them than if he had come sooner.

These feelings rapidly restored his comfort, while Mrs. Weston, of a more apprehensive disposition, foresaw nothing but a repetition of excuses and delays; and after all her concern for what her husband was to suffer, suffered a great deal more herself.

—Emma

It is dangerous to place all your hopes in another person because—human nature being what it is—he or she will *almost certainly* eventually let you down. This is shown a hundredfold in the example of Frank Churchill, who makes numerous false promises to visit his father and new stepmother at Randalls but time and again sends apologies for his delay. In a later section, Mr. Knightley will harshly criticize Frank for planting seeds of false promise and failing to come through.

No one seems to feel the sting of Frank's rudeness as sharply as Mrs. Weston, who fears that her husband is being strung along. A loyal and devoted wife, she is vexed by her husband's disappointment and ends up suffering "a great deal more herself."

If you've ever been disappointed by another person, you can understand Mrs. Weston's level of upset. We can learn from her example by choosing to believe the best about others—but making sure that our future hope is firmly rooted *only* in the one true God.

Loving fellowship with people and placing trust in them is a relational gift ordained by God, but it should never replace our need for God. On this point the apostle Paul wrote, "We . . . comfort those who are in any affliction, with the comfort with which we ourselves are comforted by God" (2 Corinthians 1:4–5). It is helpful to remember that when friends let you down—and it will happen, at some point, to everyone—you will find it easier to forgive and move forward if your trust is secure in the immovable, unchangeable love of the Savior.

While you can't know for certain that your friends will be faithful and loyal when you need them most, you *can* know that God will fill that expectation! Resolve today to be a friend who loves with a Christlike love, but seek your deepest soul-comfort in the one true Source. *He* will never let you down.

❧

OH, TASTE AND SEE THAT THE LORD IS GOOD;
BLESSED IS THE MAN WHO TAKES REFUGE IN HIM!

Psalm 34:8

Being Servant-Hearted

In all other respects, [Anne's] visit began and proceeded very well. Her own spirits improved by change of place and subject, by being removed three miles from Kellynch; Mary's ailments lessened by having a constant companion, and their daily intercourse with the other family, since there was neither superior affection, confidence, nor employment in the cottage, to be interrupted by it, was rather an advantage. It was certainly carried nearly as far as possible, for they met every morning, and hardly ever spent an evening asunder; but she believed they should not have done so well without the sight of Mr and Mrs Musgrove's respectable forms in the usual places, or without the talking, laughing, and singing of their daughters.

She played a great deal better than either of the Miss Musgroves, but having no voice, no knowledge of the harp, and no fond parents, to sit by and fancy themselves delighted, her performance was little thought of, only out of civility, or to refresh the others, as she was well aware. She knew that when she played she was giving pleasure only to herself; but this was no new sensation. Excepting one short period of her life, she had never, since the age of fourteen, never since the loss of her dear mother, known the happiness of being listened to, or encouraged by any just appreciation or real taste. In music she had been always used to feel alone in the world; and Mr and Mrs Musgrove's fond partiality for their own daughters' performance, and total indifference to any other person's, gave her much more pleasure for their sakes, than mortification for her own.

—Persuasion

Anne Elliot's gentle character is on full display in this scene, where we see her patient care for Mary, her simple enjoyment of country living, and her expression of sincere appreciation for the musical performance of the much-lauded Miss Musgroves, despite the fact that her own (superior) playing goes unacknowledged. Anne has taught herself to be content without receiving accolades.

Such servant-heartedness evokes another character, the Bible's Ruth, who demonstrated incredible humility, self-sacrifice, and loyalty by accompanying her newly widowed mother-in-law to Bethlehem. After both their husbands were killed in battle, Ruth told Naomi firmly, "Where you go I will go, and where you stay I will stay. Your people will be my people and your God my God" (Ruth 1:16 NIV).

In *Persuasion*, Anne's humble, selfless nature eventually captures the attention of Captain Wentworth and wins his heart back. In the book of Ruth, an even more powerful story plays out: Ruth catches the eye of Boaz, a rich landowner and kinsman-redeemer who marries Ruth and draws her into the Messianic line: their son, Obed, will be King David's grandfather and a direct ancestor of Christ.

If you ever feel passed over for attention or promotions, or struggle to encourage others in areas you feel unsupported, remember this: being servant-hearted does not often yield immediate results. Rather, it is a way in which we are privileged to imitate Christ. In choosing to portray humility and obedience, we get to marvel at the miracle that *we* are rescued and redeemed—for eternity—by our own Kinsman-Redeemer.

❦

FOR GOD SO LOVED THE WORLD THAT HE GAVE HIS
ONE AND ONLY SON, THAT WHOEVER BELIEVES IN HIM
SHALL NOT PERISH BUT HAVE ETERNAL LIFE.

John 3:16 NIV

RECEIVING WISE COUNSEL

"Oh! that abominable Mr. Darcy!—My father's opinion of me does me the greatest honor; and I should be miserable to forfeit it. My father, however, is partial to Mr. Wickham . . . how can I promise to be wiser than so many of my fellow creatures if I am tempted, or how am I even to know that it would be wisdom to resist? All that I can promise you, therefore, is not to be in a hurry. I will not be in a hurry to believe myself his first object. When I am in company with him, I will not be wishing. In short, I will do my best."

"Perhaps it will be as well, if you discourage his coming here so very often. At least, you should not remind your mother of inviting him."

"As I did the other day," said Elizabeth, with a conscious smile; "very true, it will be wise in me to refrain from that. But do not imagine that he is always here so often. It is on your account that he has been so frequently invited this week. You know my mother's ideas as to the necessity of constant company for her friends. But really, and upon my honour, I will try to do what I think to be wisest; and now, I hope you are satisfied."

Her aunt assured her that she was; and Elizabeth having thanked her for the kindness of her hints, they parted; a wonderful instance of advice being given on such a point without being resented.

—Pride and Prejudice

No one enjoys being corrected, but the ability to accept wise counsel is vital to character growth. This scene offers a good example, with Elizabeth's aunt, Mrs. Gardiner, gently encouraging her niece to carefully protect her heart. To her credit, Elizabeth receives the gentle criticisms well; the two women's mutual respect for one another results in "a wonderful instance of advice being given on such a point without being resented."

For reproof to bring about change, the heart must be willing to receive it. Proverbs 9:8 tells us, "Reprove a wise man, and he will love you"; the same verse warns that if we try to help a "scoffer," he will hate us. Elizabeth clearly falls into the former category; she has a certain wisdom that goes beyond her years or experience, evident in her willingness to accept advice without getting defensive.

Of course, Elizabeth is quick to toss her head and roll her eyes when Mr. Darcy's name comes up; yet she is not so biased toward Mr. Wickham that she fails to heed her aunt's gentle warning about his coming around too often. This clearheadedness, combined with Elizabeth's warmly receiving and then acting on her aunt's advice, likely saves her great heartache when Mr. Wickham is later revealed as a scoundrel.

If you want to protect your heart like Elizabeth, posture yourself in humility. Be willing to receive gentle, godly reproof and to let it shape your choices, and you will grow in wisdom and grace.

❧

TO ONE WHO LISTENS, VALID CRITICISM
IS LIKE A GOLD EARRING OR OTHER GOLD JEWELRY.

Proverbs 25:12 NLT

Governed by Selfish Impulses

The business of finding a play that would suit everybody proved to be no trifle. . . . There were, in fact, so many things to be attended to, so many people to be pleased, so many best characters required, and, above all, such a need that the play should be at once both tragedy and comedy, that there did seem as little chance of a decision as anything pursued by youth and zeal could hold out. . . .

All the best plays were run over in vain. No piece could be proposed that did not supply somebody with a difficulty, and on one side or the other it was a continual repetition of, "Oh no, that will never do! Let us have no ranting tragedies. Too many characters. Not a tolerable woman's part in the play. Anything but that, my dear Tom. It would be impossible to fill it up. One could not expect anybody to take such a part. Nothing but buffoonery from beginning to end. That might do, perhaps, but for the low parts. If I must give my opinion, I have always thought it the most insipid play in the English language. I do not wish to make objections; I shall be happy to be of any use, but I think we could not chuse worse."

Fanny looked on and listened, not unamused to observe the selfishness which, more or less disguised, seemed to govern them all, and wondering how it would end.

—*Mansfield Park*

The residents and guests of Mansfield Park—all but Edmund and Fanny—have decided to put on a theatrical production, and each person is demanding a voice. Fanny looks on, unamused, at the show of self-impulse and selfishness playing out before her, a state of affairs that offers a bitter foretaste of how each character's storyline will turn out.

Make no mistake: the selfishness governing Maria, Julia, Tom, Yates, Henry, and Mary is a natural human tendency that none of us are immune to. It is the same temptation toward self-interest that causes spouses to stray . . . political leaders to behave unscrupulously . . . church bodies to begin infighting.

The opposite of the players' behavior can be found only in pure devotion to Christ, which naturally begets a willingness to serve others, to set aside self-interests, and to find joy in humility. To attain this, we must take on the attitude of Christ, as Paul admonished his fellow believers in Philippians 2: "Is there any encouragement from belonging to Christ? Any comfort from his love? Any fellowship together in the Spirit? Are your hearts tender and compassionate? Then make me truly happy by agreeing wholeheartedly with each other, loving one another, and working together with one mind and purpose" (vv. 1–2 NLT).

Choosing a Christlike attitude means behaving like Fanny amid the reigning chaos at Mansfield Park—allowing ourselves to be governed by God's principles, not self-impulse; electing for humility over conflict; and putting others' needs ahead of our own.

❦

DON'T BE SELFISH; DON'T TRY TO IMPRESS OTHERS.
BE HUMBLE, THINKING OF OTHERS AS BETTER THAN
YOURSELVES. DON'T LOOK OUT ONLY FOR YOUR OWN
INTERESTS, BUT TAKE AN INTEREST IN OTHERS, TOO.

Philippians 2:3–4 NLT

JEALOUSY

Emma was sorry;—to have to pay civilities to a person she did not like through three long months!—to be always doing more than she wished, and less than she ought! Why she did not like Jane Fairfax might be a difficult question to answer; Mr. Knightley had once told her it was because she saw in her the really accomplished young woman, which she wanted to be thought herself; and though the accusation had been eagerly refuted at the time, there were moments of self-examination in which her conscience could not quite acquit her. But "she could never get acquainted with her: she did not know how it was, but there was such coldness and reserve—such apparent indifference whether she pleased or not—and then, her aunt was such an eternal talker!— and she was made such a fuss with by every body!—and it had been always imagined that they were to be so intimate—because their ages were the same, every body had supposed they must be so fond of each other." These were her reasons—she had no better.

It was a dislike so little just—every imputed fault was so magnified by fancy, that she never saw Jane Fairfax the first time after any considerable absence, without feeling that she had injured her.

—Emma

Jealousy—often referred to as the "green-eyed monster"— has its hold on even Emma Woodhouse. We see this in her narrowed-eye assessment of Jane Fairfax, possibly the only Highbury resident ever to threaten Emma's standing.

Mr. Knightley correctly surmises that Emma sees in Jane that "which she wanted to be thought herself." But Emma would rather list the things she doesn't care for in Jane: she is too reserved, too fussed over, has too chatty an aunt. The greatest insult, however, seems to be that everyone assumes a friendship merely from their likeness in age. The nerve!

Unfortunately, Emma displays a spiritual immaturity that many of us may relate to. Paul referred to it in 1 Corinthians 3:1–3 when he said, "Brothers, I could not address you as spiritual but as worldly—*mere infants in Christ.* I gave you milk, not solid food, for you were not yet ready for it. Indeed, you are still not ready. You are still worldly. For since there is jealousy and quarreling among you, are you not worldly?" (NIV, emphasis added).

The kind of "jealousy and quarreling" on display by these early Christians is not unlike what we see in Emma: it is childish, self-centered, impatient, and insecure—the willful actions of a defiant child who wants her way. Worse, it creates a mind-set that distances us from being in right relationship with God; a line of thinking that cannot be changed until we surrender it to Him.

Does jealousy sometimes rise up in you, unbidden? Do you need God to reshape your heart? Focus on who God created *you* to be—not your neighbor, or your friend, or your competition. He gave you a glorious identity in Him; let Him transform your thinking with this knowledge!

❦

ONE THING I DO: FORGETTING WHAT LIES BEHIND AND STRAINING FORWARD TO WHAT LIES AHEAD, I PRESS ON TOWARD THE GOAL FOR THE PRIZE OF THE UPWARD CALL OF GOD IN CHRIST JESUS.

Phillipians 3:13–14

FORSAKING THE LONG-TERM PRIZE

When the gentlemen had joined them, and tea was over, the card tables were placed. Lady Catherine, Sir William, and Mr. and Mrs. Collins sat down to quadrille; and as Miss De Bourgh chose to play at cassino, the two girls had the honour of assisting Mrs. Jenkinson to make up her party. Their table was superlatively stupid. Scarcely a syllable was uttered that did not relate to the game, except when Mrs. Jenkinson expressed her fears of Miss De Bourgh's being too hot or too cold, or having too much or too little light. A great deal more passed at the other table, Lady Catherine was generally speaking—stating the mistakes of the three others, or relating some anecdote of herself. Mr. Collins was employed in agreeing to every thing her Ladyship said, thanking her for every fish he won, and apologising if he thought he won too many. Sir William did not say much. He was storing his memory with anecdotes and noble names.

When Lady Catherine and her daughter had played as long as they chose, the tables were broke up, the carriage was offered to Mrs. Collins, gratefully accepted, and immediately ordered. The party then gathered round the fire to hear Lady Catherine determine what weather they were to have on the morrow. From these instructions they were summoned by the arrival of the coach, and with many speeches of thankfulness on Mr. Collins's side, and as many bows on Sir William's, they departed. As soon as they had driven from the door, Elizabeth was called on by her cousin to give her opinion of all that she had seen at Rosings, which, for Charlotte's sake, she made more favourable than it really was. But her commendation, though costing her some trouble, could by no means satisfy Mr. Collins, and he was very soon obliged to take her ladyship's praise into his own hands.

—Pride and Prejudice

Finally, we meet the infamous Lady Catherine de Bourgh. In this scene, she is holding court at a dinner party given in her enormous home. In short order we realize that Lady Catherine's reputation is richly deserved: she is a meddlesome, opinionated know-it-all who happens to have more money than she knows what to do with. Even worse, she is surrounded by obsequious fools like Mr. Collins—devoted admirers who hang on her every word and are grateful for crumbs of recognition.

Lady Catherine is what the Bible would call a "rich fool," a state of being that is frequently shown in the Bible as one of the biggest impediments to living a rich, full life for Christ. In the parable of the rich fool, Jesus talked about a rich man who wanted to gain as much wealth as possible so that he could live an easy life; but when he died soon thereafter, his storehouse of goods did nothing for him: "God said to him, 'Fool! This night your soul is required of you, and the things you have prepared, whose will they be?' So is the one who lays up treasure for himself and is not rich toward God" (Luke 12:20–21).

We often see in people like Lady Catherine a selfish enjoyment of short-term pleasures, like owning things and controlling those around them. Yet none of it counts toward the real prize—eternity with the Father.

৶৽৽

SO DON'T BE DISMAYED WHEN THE WICKED GROW RICH
AND THEIR HOMES BECOME EVER MORE SPLENDID.
FOR WHEN THEY DIE, THEY TAKE NOTHING WITH THEM.
THEIR WEALTH WILL NOT FOLLOW THEM INTO THE GRAVE.
IN THIS LIFE THEY CONSIDER THEMSELVES FORTUNATE
AND ARE APPLAUDED FOR THEIR SUCCESS.

Psalm 49:16–18 NLT

Striving for Pure Motives

"Indeed you wrong me," replied Lucy, with great solemnity; "I know nobody of whose judgment I think so highly as I do of yours; and I do really believe, that if you was to say to me, 'I advise you by all means to put an end to your engagement with Edward Ferrars, it will be more for the happiness of both of you,' I should resolve upon doing it immediately."

Elinor blushed for the insincerity of Edward's future wife, and replied, "This compliment would effectually frighten me from giving any opinion on the subject had I formed one. It raises my influence much too high; the power of dividing two people so tenderly attached is too much for an indifferent person."

"'Tis because you are an indifferent person," said Lucy, with some pique, and laying a particular stress on those words, "that your judgment might justly have such weight with me. If you could be supposed to be biased in any respect by your own feelings, your opinion would not be worth having."

Elinor thought it wisest to make no answer to this, lest they might provoke each other to an unsuitable increase of ease and unreserve; and was even partly determined never to mention the subject again.

Another pause therefore of many minutes' duration, succeeded this speech, and Lucy was still the first to end it.

—Sense and Sensibility

Lucy Steele is taunting poor Elinor about Lucy's so-called secret engagement to Edward Ferrars. "I value no one's opinion higher than yours, Elinor!" Lucy cries, and you can almost see her eyes widening in feigned innocence. But Elinor sees through Lucy's shallow praise and bristles at the hypocrisy. Edward deserves better.

This hearkens to a well-known dispute in 1 Kings 3:16–28, where two women are brought before King Solomon. Both are claiming ownership of a baby boy, but only one is the true mother. To decide the matter, Solomon orders that the baby be split in half:

> The woman whose son was alive was filled with compassion for her son and said to the king, "Please, my lord, give her the living baby! Don't kill him!"
>
> But the other said, "Neither I nor you shall have him. Cut him in two!"
>
> Then the king gave his ruling: "Give the living baby to the first woman. Do not kill him; she is his mother."
> (vv. 26–27 NIV)

Note the difference: The instinct of the true mother is to protect her child. Meanwhile, the liar—in her bitter jealousy—is undone.

Likewise, a jealous Lucy does not really love Edward, but she will do anything to keep him from Elinor (or Elinor from him). Her motives are, at best, insincere. Elinor, on the other hand, would rather see Edward betrothed to a woman of character—a woman who esteems his virtues and has his best interests at heart—than a manipulative future wife. Her motive is pure.

Acting in love often requires self-sacrifice. Strive to be free of impure motives in your dealings with others; you will honor the Lord and receive the reward of His pleasure.

❧

SEARCH ME, O GOD, AND KNOW MY HEART;
TRY ME, AND KNOW MY ANXIETIES;
AND SEE IF THERE IS ANY WICKED WAY IN ME,
AND LEAD ME IN THE WAY EVERLASTING.

Psalm 139:23–24 NKJV

JUSTIFYING COMPROMISE

"We see things very differently," cried Maria. "I am perfectly acquainted with the play, I assure you; and with a very few omissions, and so forth, which will be made, of course, I can see nothing objectionable in it; and I am not the only young woman you find who thinks it very fit for private representation."

"I am sorry for it," was [Edmund's] answer; "but in this matter it is you who are to lead. You must set the example. If others have blundered, it is your place to put them right, and shew them what true delicacy is. In all points of decorum your conduct must be law to the rest of the party."

This picture of her consequence had some effect, for no one loved better to lead than Maria; and with far more good-humour she answered, "I am much obliged to you, Edmund; you mean very well, I am sure: but I still think you see things too strongly; and I really cannot undertake to harangue all the rest upon a subject of this kind. There would be the greatest indecorum, I think."

"Do you imagine that I could have such an idea in my head? No; let your conduct be the only harangue. Say that, on examining the part, you feel yourself unequal to it; that you find it requiring more exertion and confidence than you can be supposed to have. Say this with firmness, and it will be quite enough. All who can distinguish will understand your motive. The play will be given up, and your delicacy honoured as it ought."

—Mansfield Park

Edmund disapproves of the play *Lovers' Vows* for two reasons: it promotes a kind of gaiety that is improper in his father's absence, and the lascivious written material is inappropriate. So Edmund appeals to Maria, as the eldest Bertram, to take the moral high ground. Though she is flattered—"for no one loved better to lead than Maria"—his argument falls on deaf ears. Edmund does not know that hidden sin in Maria's heart overrules any moral implications.

Our hidden sins are often what tempt us to make wrong decisions, or that keep us from making the right ones. In Maria's case, temptation comes in the form of an opportunity to play the romantic lead opposite Henry Crawford. Under the guise of playacting, Maria will get to act the role of Henry's lover, something she craves even though she is engaged to Mr. Rushworth. Maria either fails to recognize or does not care that she is trading her future for a series of in-the-moment pleasures.

Allowing our emotions to dictate our actions is something we all struggle with—probably more than we care to admit! And our impure motives too often disqualify us as the best judge of a situation. As Jesus told His disciples, "You're not in the driver's seat; I am. . . . Self-help is no help at all. Self-sacrifice is the way, my way, to finding yourself, your true self. What kind of deal is it to get everything you want but lose yourself?" (Matthew 16:24–26 MSG).

We're such poor choosers when it comes to ourselves— we think in the moment and act myopically. Throughout His ministry, Jesus showed His followers that the only way to kill this habit is to relinquish all authority to Him. Like the disciples, choose Jesus—and resolve to follow the same path.

❧

"AND WHAT DO YOU BENEFIT IF YOU GAIN THE WHOLE
WORLD BUT LOSE YOUR OWN SOUL?"

Mark 8:36 NLT

Chasing Out "Little Foxes"

She studied every sentence: and her feelings towards its writer were at times widely different. When she remembered the style of his address, she was still full of indignation; but when she considered how unjustly she had condemned and upbraided him, her anger was turned against herself; and his disappointed feelings became the object of compassion. His attachment excited gratitude, his general character respect; but she could not approve him; nor could she for a moment repent her refusal, or feel the slightest inclination ever to see him again.

In her own past behaviour, there was a constant source of vexation and regret; and in the unhappy defects of her family a subject of yet heavier chagrin. They were hopeless of remedy. Her father, contented with laughing at them, would never exert himself to restrain the wild giddiness of his youngest daughters; and her mother, with manners so far from right herself, was entirely insensible of the evil. Elizabeth had frequently united with Jane in an endeavour to check the imprudence of Catherine and Lydia; but while they were supported by their mother's indulgence, what chance could there be of improvement? Catherine, weak-spirited, irritable, and completely under Lydia's guidance, had been always affronted by their advice; and Lydia, self-willed and careless, would scarcely give them a hearing. They were ignorant, idle, and vain. While there was an officer in Meryton, they would flirt with him; and while Meryton was within a walk of Longbourn, they would be going there for ever.

—*Pride and Prejudice*

lizabeth is deeply conflicted. A large portion of Mr. Darcy's letter is devoted to explaining why he is repulsed by most of her family—specifically, her younger sisters and both her parents. Elizabeth's familial loyalty cannot withstand the knowledge that Mr. Darcy is right: her father is too amused by his younger daughters' ridiculous antics to discipline them; her mother is insensible and silly herself; and the three girls are a blend of imprudence, weak-spiritedness, irritability, unwillingness to accept advice, self-will, and carelessness.

A verse in Song of Solomon addresses the kind of spoilage we see in these characters. "Catch us the foxes, the little foxes that spoil the vines, for our vines have tender grapes" (2:15 NKJV). The term *little foxes* here refers to small things—seemingly insignificant words, actions, and habits—that can lead to major damage in our lives. It is derived from the idea of what foxes do to a vineyard. Little foxes, too small to reach the grapes, would chew on the hanging leaves and lowest vines. As a result, a farmer loses not just his crop, but entire vines—a far worse consequence.

The spiritual lesson for us is that any little thing we allow or practice can ultimately prove disastrous to our character. The youngest Bennet girls did not become flirtatious, silly, slovenly, and lazy overnight. These attitudes and qualities were fostered in tiny ways throughout their lives, as their father became more distant and their mother more indulgent. In time, girlish propensities morphed into vanity and obsessive flirtations.

It may be as simple as a particular indulgence, an unhealthy idea you nurture, or constantly putting off your quiet time with the Lord; undealt with, any of these can lead to poverty of spirit. So be on your guard against whatever might steal your goal of living like Christ.

❦

A LITTLE SLEEP, A LITTLE SLUMBER,
A LITTLE FOLDING OF THE HANDS TO REST—
AND POVERTY WILL COME ON YOU LIKE A BANDIT
AND SCARCITY LIKE AN ARMED MAN.

Proverbs 24:33–34 NIV

Adoption into God's Family

Such was Jane Fairfax's history. She had fallen into good hands, known nothing but kindness from the Campbells, and been given an excellent education. Living constantly with right-minded and well-informed people, her heart and understanding had received every advantage of discipline and culture; and Colonel Campbell's residence being in London, every lighter talent had been done full justice to, by the attendance of first-rate masters. Her disposition and abilities were equally worthy of all that friendship could do; and at eighteen or nineteen she was, as far as such an early age can be qualified for the care of children, fully competent to the office of instruction herself; but she was too much beloved to be parted with. Neither father nor mother could promote, and the daughter could not endure it. The evil day was put off. It was easy to decide that she was still too young; and Jane remained with them, sharing, as another daughter, in all the rational pleasures of an elegant society, and a judicious mixture of home and amusement, with only the drawback of the future, the sobering suggestions of her own good understanding to remind her that all this might soon be over. The affection of the whole family, the warm attachment of Miss Campbell in particular, was the more honourable to each party from the circumstance of Jane's decided superiority both in beauty and acquirements.

—Emma

The evidences of the Campbell family's good influence on Jane Fairfax are many: she is right-minded and well-informed, disciplined and cultured. She has received every advantage from being raised by them, including the affection and warmth of genuine attachment. She may be an orphan, but Jane has been given a family—and the blessing and good effects of this gift are evident in her countenance, her manners, and her carriage.

We too are adopted—as Christians, we are "grafted in" to the Vine. This process begins when we enter into relationship with Christ: immediately we benefit from becoming part of His family!

In the parable of the vine and the branches, Jesus shared what this looks like with His followers: "I am the vine; you are the branches. Whoever abides in me and I in him, he it is that bears much fruit, for apart from me you can do nothing" (John 15:5).

When we "abide" with Him, we start taking on characteristics of the new life flowing through us—the inward evidence of His influence and the indwelling work of His Spirit. The "fruit" Jesus spoke of is the outward change that comes as a result of adoption into His family. As happened with Jane Fairfax, we receive the many benefits of living lives aligned with His goodness and righteousness. His desires become our desires; His plans for us become plans of our own. We are literally shaped by Him as we allow His influence into every area of our lives.

❧

"ABIDE IN ME, AND I IN YOU. AS THE BRANCH CANNOT
BEAR FRUIT BY ITSELF, UNLESS IT ABIDES IN THE VINE,
NEITHER CAN YOU, UNLESS YOU ABIDE IN ME."

John 15:4

"It is very charming indeed," said Isabella, with a grave face.

"Mr. Morland has behaved vastly handsome indeed," said the gentle Mrs. Thorpe, looking anxiously at her daughter. "I only wish I could do as much. One could not expect more from him, you know. If he finds he can do more by and by, I dare say he will, for I am sure he must be an excellent good-hearted man. Four hundred is but a small income to begin on indeed, but your wishes, my dear Isabella, are so moderate, you do not consider how little you ever want, my dear."

"It is not on my own account I wish for more; but I cannot bear to be the means of injuring my dear Morland, making him sit down upon an income hardly enough to find one in the common necessaries of life. For myself, it is nothing; I never think of myself."

"I know you never do, my dear; and you will always find your reward in the affection it makes everybody feel for you. There never was a young woman so beloved as you are by everybody that knows you; and I dare say when Mr. Morland sees you, my dear child—but do not let us distress our dear Catherine by talking of such things. Mr. Morland has behaved so very handsome, you know. I always heard he was a most excellent man; and you know, my dear, we are not to suppose but what, if you had had a suitable fortune, he would have come down with something more, for I am sure he must be a most liberal-minded man."

—*Northanger Abbey*

Newly engaged Isabella is disappointed—and money is the cause. The amount she and James will have to live on is less than she expected, and her bitter disappointment is evident, though she pretends her concern is for her fiancé: "For myself, it is nothing; I never think of myself."

In Luke 12, Jesus explains to us why Isabella's misplaced emphasis on money is not just wrong, but foolish: "Be on your guard against all covetousness, for one's life does not consist in the abundance of his possessions" (v. 15). Jesus goes on to share with His disciples the parable of the rich fool and reveals one of the great weaknesses of the human heart—that the more we gain, the greater our appetite.

Isabella wanted only to marry James but is now petulant and unhappy at the thought of a less-than-comfortable life-style. This same unhappiness creeps into our hearts when we focus on what we *don't have*: the clothes, the vacations, the house or car or job. The life we see others enjoying and think we deserve! The only way to prevent discontent from taking hold in our lives is to actively, daily profess thanks for everything we *do* have—and to assign this gratitude to its Source, the Giver of all good gifts.

Don't focus on things you don't have. Be thankful for the abundance you've been blessed with! Gratitude is a surefire greed killer.

⊷

GIVE THANKS IN ALL CIRCUMSTANCES; FOR THIS IS
THE WILL OF GOD IN CHRIST JESUS FOR YOU.

1 Thessalonians 5:18

TAMING THE TONGUE

"Now I have got some news for you," said Lydia, as they sat down to table. "What do you think? It is excellent news, capital news, and about a certain person that we all like."

Jane and Elizabeth looked at each other, and the waiter was told that he need not stay. Lydia laughed, and said, "Aye, that is just like your formality and discretion. You thought the waiter must not hear, as if he cared! I dare say he often hears worse things said than I am going to say. But he is an ugly fellow! I am glad he is gone. I never saw such a long chin in my life. Well, but now for my news: it is about dear Wickham; too good for the waiter, is not it? There is no danger of Wickham's marrying Mary King. There's for you! She is gone down to her uncle at Liverpool; gone to stay. Wickham is safe."

"And Mary King is safe!" added Elizabeth; "safe from a connection imprudent as to fortune."

"She is a great fool for going away, if she liked him."

"But I hope there is no strong attachment on either side," said Jane.

"I am sure there is not on his. I will answer for it he never cared three straws about her. Who could about such a nasty little freckled thing?"

—Pride and Prejudice

In this scene we are exposed to the most shocking example yet of Lydia's crude, thoughtless behavior. First, she scorns her older sisters' discretion in sending the waiter away before she launches into full-fledged gossip; then she calls Mr. Wickham's most recent love interest a "nasty little freckled thing." Her words paint a vivid picture of a young woman obsessed with image, boys, and cutting down whomever she considers less important than herself.

It seems clear that everything Lydia says and does is focused on what will bring her the most immediate satisfaction. In Matthew 12:35, we are reminded that the words passing our lips are *always* representative of what rules our hearts: "The good person out of his good treasure brings forth good, and the evil person out of his evil treasure brings forth evil." Lydia's flippant speeches reveal a heart filled not with "godly treasure" but "evil treasure." Is it any wonder? She is fifteen, the petted baby of the family, and has been raised by a mother who, through example, encouraged attitudes of laziness and self-gratification.

Do you justify speaking certain words that you know aren't pleasing to God? Do you speak before you think, and repent later? If you want to create pure streams of living water in your heart, you must surrender your right to say whatever you want. Let God's gentle guidance in the area of your speech create in you a heart He is proud to call home.

❦

LET THE WORDS OF MY MOUTH
AND THE MEDITATION OF MY HEART
BE ACCEPTABLE IN YOUR SIGHT,
O LORD, MY ROCK AND MY REDEEMER.

Psalm 19:14

NURSING ENVY

Julia did suffer, however, though Mrs. Grant discerned it not, and though it escaped the notice of many of her own family likewise. She had loved [Henry Crawford], she did love still, and she had all the suffering which a warm temper and a high spirit were likely to endure under the disappointment of a dear, though irrational hope, with a strong sense of ill-usage. Her heart was sore and angry, and she was capable only of angry consolations. The sister with whom she was used to be on easy terms was now become her greatest enemy: they were alienated from each other; and Julia was not superior to the hope of some distressing end to the attentions which were still carrying on there, some punishment to Maria for conduct so shameful towards herself as well as towards Mr. Rushworth. With no material fault of temper, or difference of opinion, to prevent their being very good friends while their interests were the same, the sisters, under such a trial as this, had not affection or principle enough to make them merciful or just, to give them honour or compassion. Maria felt her triumph, and pursued her purpose, careless of Julia; and Julia could never see Maria distinguished by Henry Crawford without trusting that it would create jealousy, and bring a public disturbance at last.

—Mansfield Park

The ongoing rivalry between Maria and Julia is due to jealousy over Henry Crawford. Equally determined to gain his attention, the normally affectionate sisters have become bitter rivals who, "under such a trial as this, had not affection or principle enough to make them merciful or just, to give them honour or compassion." In other words, their rivalry has tested their devotion as sisters, and each wants to see the other lose.

Envy and resentment are ugly emotions; add self-interest and self-ambition to the mix, and it becomes a recipe for turning on each other. One of the oldest and best-known examples can be found in the story of the first brothers: Abel, a shepherd, and Cain, a farmer. When each offered his sacrifice to the Lord, Abel's was preferred. Jealous over this, Cain acted in rage: "And when they were in the field, Cain rose up against his brother Abel and killed him" (Genesis 4:8). Killed his own brother, because God showed him favor!

Where jealousy is unresolved, it leads to bitterness. In relationships, this bitterness can bring about strife, division, and even generations of feuding—all because the Christian goals of serving and meeting each other's needs are surpassed by selfishness and a desire to control.

To eradicate jealousy, we have to desire godliness more than we want vindication, approval, or recognition—whatever sinful motive is driving our hearts. If you're struggling with this sin, confess it to God and ask Him to remove any jealous hurt from your heart. Gradually, it will be replaced by reminders of God's unfailing love and acceptance.

❧

IF WE CONFESS OUR SINS, HE IS FAITHFUL AND JUST TO
FORGIVE US OUR SINS AND TO CLEANSE US FROM ALL
UNRIGHTEOUSNESS.

1 John 1:9

BEHAVING NOBLY

They were three days on their journey, and Marianne's behaviour as they travelled was a happy specimen of what future complaisance and companionableness to Mrs. Jennings might be expected to be. She sat in silence almost all the way, wrapt in her own meditations, and scarcely ever voluntarily speaking, except when any object of picturesque beauty within their view drew from her an exclamation of delight exclusively addressed to her sister.

To atone for this conduct therefore, Elinor took immediate possession of the post of civility which she had assigned herself, behaved with the greatest attention to Mrs. Jennings, talked with her, laughed with her, and listened to her whenever she could; and Mrs. Jennings on her side treated them both with all possible kindness, was solicitous on every occasion for their ease and enjoyment, and only disturbed that she could not make them choose their own dinners at the inn, nor extort a confession of their preferring salmon to cod, or boiled fowls to veal cutlets. They reached town by three o'clock the third day, glad to be released, after such a journey, from the confinement of a carriage, and ready to enjoy all the luxury of a good fire.

—*Sense and Sensibility*

In the mid-1700s, a three-day journey by stagecoach would be exhausting. For Elinor, the wearying effects of the trip are compounded by Marianne's behavior: her singular, passionate focus (reuniting with Willoughby) and total disregard for their kindly host, Mrs. Jennings.

Anything that strikes Marianne's fancy is celebrated and delighted over; by contrast, whatever disinterests or fails to amuse her receives no recognition whatsoever. It is a defect in her character that Elinor will often sigh about in the pages to come, then quietly attempt to atone for without drawing attention to her sister.

We are told that to compensate, Elinor takes "immediate possession of the post of civility which she had assigned herself." This renders Elinor's behavior "civil" —by definition, proper, polite, respectful, and thinking of others before herself. Civility might also be defined as the *opposite* of Marianne's behavior, for civility puts others' interests ahead of one's own.

Self-interest rules our lives in far more ways than we want to admit. Even the apostle Peter, who professed his love for Christ with a passion equal to Marianne's, denied Him thrice before the rooster crowed!

For the most stunning example of true civility, look to the One who modeled it best: Jesus Christ. Though blameless, He bore our sins on the cross to pay the debt for our forgiveness. Was any sacrifice ever so others-centered?

◈

BUT HE WAS PIERCED FOR OUR TRANSGRESSIONS,

HE WAS CRUSHED FOR OUR INIQUITIES;

THE PUNISHMENT THAT BROUGHT US PEACE WAS UPON HIM,

AND BY HIS WOUNDS WE ARE HEALED.

Isaiah 53:5 NIV

SACRIFICES IN PARENTING

Had Elizabeth's opinion been all drawn from her own family, she could not have formed a very pleasing picture of conjugal felicity or domestic comfort. Her father, captivated by youth and beauty, and that appearance of good humour which youth and beauty generally give, had married a woman whose weak understanding and illiberal mind had, very early in their marriage, put an end to all real affection for her. Respect, esteem, and confidence had vanished for ever; and all his views of domestic happiness were overthrown. But Mr. Bennet was not of a disposition to seek comfort, for the disappointment which his own imprudence had brought on, in any of those pleasures which too often console the unfortunate for their folly or their vice. He was fond of the country and of books; and from these tastes had arisen his principal enjoyments.

Elizabeth, however, had never been blind to the impropriety of her father's behaviour as a husband. She had always seen it with pain; but respecting his abilities, and grateful for his affectionate treatment of herself, she endeavoured to forget what she could not overlook, and to banish from her thoughts that continual breach of conjugal obligation and decorum which, in exposing his wife to the contempt of her own children, was so highly reprehensible. But she had never felt so strongly as now the disadvantages which must attend the children of so unsuitable a marriage, nor ever been so fully aware of the evils arising from so ill-judged a direction of talents; talents which rightly used, might at least have preserved the respectability of his daughters, even if incapable of enlarging the mind of his wife.

—*Pride and Prejudice*

At first glance, it seems as if there is a certain nobility at play here: Mr. Bennet has made the best of an unhappy marriage. But the dark side is that his hands-off approach equates lazy parenting. Too little governance, it turns out, leads to willfulness and rebellion in Lydia. His decision to let her accompany the Forsters to Brighton—a choice from which Elizabeth tries to dissuade him—will turn out to be a grave mistake.

It's a sobering reminder that as parents, we have to live out the gospel for our children. In order to do this, we first must have a sound personal relationship with Christ. In other words, we must willingly follow Him with our whole hearts before we can begin to lead our children successfully.

As wives and mothers, we know that raising children in the ways of the Lord requires gospel-saturated living—letting Scripture be our guide, not our own hearts or inclinations. When we live this way, we'll be able to make the difficult decisions, even when we're tired or fed up—saying no to requests like Lydia's; correcting our children's behavior on a heart level; freely sacrificing our time and energy to create a warm and loving home; carving out ways for our children to enjoy creation and use their God-given imaginations; and most of all, praying fervently that they would be drawn into loving relationship with the Savior.

Mr. Bennet's self-postured parenting became his default mode, and it led to Lydia's disgrace. But you and I can make different choices—choices that reflect on-mission parenting, to the glory of God; godly choices that reverberate in the hearts of our children. Choices that carry *huge* spiritual impact for future generations.

❦

CHILDREN ARE A HERITAGE FROM THE LORD.

Psalm 127:3

SPIRITUAL HYPOCHONDRIA

[When] Anne enquired after Captain Benwick, Mary's face was clouded directly. Charles laughed.

"Oh! Captain Benwick is very well, I believe, but he is a very odd young man. I do not know what he would be at." . . .

Charles laughed again and said, "Now Mary, you know very well how it really was. It was all your doing," (turning to Anne.) "He fancied that if he went with us, he should find you close by: he fancied everybody to be living in Uppercross; and when he discovered that Lady Russell lived three miles off, his heart failed him, and he had not courage to come. That is the fact, upon my honour, Mary knows it is."

But Mary did not give into it very graciously, whether from not considering Captain Benwick entitled by birth and situation to be in love with an Elliot, or from not wanting to believe Anne a greater attraction to Uppercross than herself, must be left to be guessed. Anne's good-will, however, was not to be lessened by what she heard. She boldly acknowledged herself flattered, and continued her enquiries.

"Oh! he talks of you," cried Charles, "in such terms—"

Mary interrupted him. "I declare, Charles, I never heard him mention Anne twice all the time I was there. I declare, Anne, he never talks of you at all."

—*Persuasion*

The character of Mary Elliot lives in a small world of her own making. If she is not complaining loudly about how some women neglect their children, she is devising ways to leave her own at home. If her husband does not pay her enough attention, she languishes on the couch, claiming that no one ever suffered the half of what she does. And though she is a married woman, she cannot bear to have another woman receive attention from eligible bachelors, even if the "other woman" is her own sweet sister Anne.

Mary suffers from a condition known as *glory seeking*, in which her world revolves around her, and her jealous machinations are painfully obvious to the reader. That she does not recognize this herself is further evidence of how self-consumed she has become.

A perfect contrast to Mary is on display in the missionary journeys of Paul and Silas, who in 1 Thessalonians took the gospel to Thessalonica with the singular pursuit of bringing men and women to Christ. Paul and Silas were not the center of their universe; the Lord was! Nor were they interested in seeking glory for themselves. So driven were these men to exhibit God's glory that they spoke "as messengers approved by God to be entrusted with the Good News. Our purpose is to please God, not people. He alone examines the motives of our hearts" (2:4 NLT).

It is not wrong to seek glory; the question is whether you're looking for it from others or from the Lord. One does not even compare to the other!

❦

HE CALLED YOU TO SALVATION WHEN WE TOLD YOU THE GOOD NEWS; NOW YOU CAN SHARE IN THE GLORY OF OUR LORD JESUS CHRIST.

2 Thessalonians 2:14 NLT

POWER OF A WELL-PLACED WORD

Fanny, in her pity and kindheartedness, was at great pains to teach [Mr. Rushworth] how to learn, giving him all the helps and directions in her power, trying to make an artificial memory for him, and learning every word of his part herself, but without his being much the forwarder.

Many uncomfortable, anxious, apprehensive feelings she certainly had; but with all these, and other claims on her time and attention, she was as far from finding herself without employment or utility amongst them, as without a companion in uneasiness; quite as far from having no demand on her leisure as on her compassion. The gloom of her first anticipations was proved to have been unfounded. She was occasionally useful to all; she was perhaps as much at peace as any.

There was a great deal of needlework to be done, moreover, in which her help was wanted; and that Mrs. Norris thought her quite as well off as the rest, was evident by the manner in which she claimed it—"Come, Fanny," she cried, "these are fine times for you, but you must not be always walking from one room to the other, and doing the lookings—on at your ease, in this way; I want you here." . . .

Fanny took the work very quietly, without attempting any defence.

—*Mansfield Park*

ere, we get a glimpse of Fanny's gentle nature as she tries to help Mr. Rushworth learn his lines for the play; through Fanny's helpful, patient coaching and encouragement he begins to cover ground. Then moments later, Fanny is berated by Aunt Norris—an unjust accusation—and given a basketful of needlework to finish. True to her nature, Fanny takes it up quietly.

In *Mansfield Park,* every other female character is quick to speak her mind, easily angered, and puts voice to whatever she thinks. Not Fanny: she knows the value in holding her tongue, observing keenly, and inserting her opinion when it will do the most good.

Building character in this way does not come naturally. However, it's important to remember that in every encounter in our lives, we are God's representatives; as such, we must choose our words carefully. We also have to become thoughtful and selective not just about *what* we say, but also *how* and *when* we speak.

It is always a good idea to stop, think, and pray before responding. Ask the Lord for wisdom, like the psalmist who prayed, "Let the words of my mouth and the meditation of my heart be acceptable in Your sight, O LORD, my strength and my Redeemer" (Psalm 19:14 NKJV).

Do you struggle to hold your tongue? Perhaps you are quick to criticize, correct, or gossip. Ask God to help you discern the correct response, or even no response; let Him become the guide of your heart and thoughts before you speak.

❦

THE PREPARATION OF THE HEART BELONGS TO MAN,
BUT THE ANSWER OF THE TONGUE IS FROM THE LORD.

Proverbs 16:1 NKJV

LOOKING FOR WAYS TO SERVE

"He is the best landlord, and the best master," said [Mr. Darcy's house-keeper, Mrs. Reynolds], "that ever lived. Not like the wild young men now-a-days, who think of nothing but themselves. There is not one of his tenants or servants but what will give him a good name. Some people call him proud; but I am sure I never saw any thing of it. To my fancy, it is only because he does not rattle away like other young men."

"In what an amiable light does this place him!" thought Elizabeth. . . .

There was certainly at this moment, in Elizabeth's mind, a more gentle sensation towards the original than she had ever felt in the height of their acquaintance. The commendation bestowed on him by Mrs. Reynolds was of no trifling nature. What praise is more valuable than the praise of an intelligent servant? As a brother, a landlord, a master, she considered how many people's happiness were in his guardianship!—How much of pleasure or pain it was in his power to bestow!—How much of good or evil must be done by him! Every idea that had been brought forward by the housekeeper was favourable to his character, and as she stood before the canvas, on which he was represented, and fixed his eyes upon herself, she thought of his regard with a deeper sentiment of gratitude than it had ever raised before; she remembered its warmth, and softened its impropriety of expression.

—Pride and Prejudice

Here, through the eyes of Mrs. Reynolds, the house-keeper at Pemberley, Elizabeth has glimpsed a whole new side to Mr. Darcy . . . and she is astonished. "He is the best landlord, and the best master that ever lived," Mrs.

Reynolds tells her visitors earnestly. "Some people call him proud; but I am sure I never saw any thing of it . . . it is only because he does not rattle away like other young men."

This insider's view is one of the turning points in Darcy and Elizabeth's love story. As Elizabeth wisely observes, the manner in which a servant speaks of her master is reflective of his true character, and in this she is given proof of something she long suspected: Mr Darcy's so-called proud behavior is not exactly what it appears. Through Mrs. Reynolds's praise of Darcy as a master, an estate owner, and a brother, Elizabeth begins to perceive Darcy's real merits—his true nature as he reveals it to those closest to him. It is an illuminating glimpse of a man who leads his staff and family in love.

This same kind of servant leadership is what God calls us to. To understand what it looks like, we have the greatest example in human history: Jesus, who left the beauty and majesty of heaven to "empty" Himself by taking on the form of a servant. Philippians 2:8 tells us, "And being found in human form, he humbled himself by becoming obedient to the point of death, even death on a cross."

In His time on earth, Jesus was *always* looking for opportunities to serve and bless and love and encourage those around Him, and we are called to do the same. Through His example, we get to see what true greatness looks like. If you desire to become great in God's kingdom, then you must learn to be the servant of all.

❧

"THE GREATEST AMONG YOU SHALL BE YOUR SERVANT.
WHOEVER EXALTS HIMSELF WILL BE HUMBLED, AND
WHOEVER HUMBLES HIMSELF WILL BE EXALTED."

Matthew 23:11–12

THE FIRST BEATITUDE

Harriet . . . had seen only Mrs. Martin and the two girls. They had received her doubtingly, if not coolly; and nothing beyond the merest commonplace had been talked almost all the time—till just at last, when Mrs. Martin's saying, all of a sudden, that she thought Miss Smith was grown, had brought on a more interesting subject, and a warmer manner. In that very room she had been measured last September, with her two friends. There were the pencilled marks and memorandums on the wainscot by the window. He had done it. They all seemed to remember the day, the hour, the party, the occasion—to feel the same consciousness, the same regrets—to be ready to return to the same good understanding; and they were just growing again like themselves, (Harriet, as Emma must suspect, as ready as the best of them to be cordial and happy,) when the carriage reappeared, and all was over. . . .

It was a bad business. [Emma] would have given a great deal, or endured a great deal, to have had the Martins in a higher rank of life. They were so deserving, that a little higher should have been enough: but as it was, how could she have done otherwise?—Impossible!—She could not repent. They must be separated; but there was a great deal of pain in the process—so much to herself at this time, that she soon felt the necessity of a little consolation, and resolved on going home by way of Randalls to procure it.

—*Emma*

mma has critically evaluated the Martins, and found them lacking. Oh, she *wishes* that they held a higher status in society, for Harriet's sake—her sincerity in this is evident: "They were so deserving, that a *little* higher should have been enough." She sees and even appreciates the many good qualities of the Martin family, but her high standard for her friend, as ridiculous as it is far-reaching, will not be moved. That this inconveniences no one more than Emma herself is simple justice.

Throughout *Emma*, we watch Mr. Martin, his mother, and his sisters exemplify the biblical ideals of humility and meekness—qualities so vital to spiritual maturity that they make up the first beatitude in Jesus' Sermon on the Mount: "And he opened his mouth and taught them, saying: 'Blessed are the *poor in spirit*, for theirs is the kingdom of heaven'" (Matthew 5:2–3, emphasis added).

The word *beatitude* stems from a Latin word that means "happiness." Being "poor in spirit" is one of the ways to develop close relationship with Christ and experience happiness in its purest form on earth, as well as gain an eternal inheritance. It's an upside-down logic that Jesus calls us to.

It will be a long journey before Emma eventually accepts and finally embraces Harriet's match with Mr. Martin—but when she does, it is an indication that she has matured in her thinking, and perhaps grown a little in her faith.

When you foster haughtiness in your heart, you are cheating only yourself—of genuine happiness. Pray about what being "poor in spirit" means for you and the changes in attitudes and actions you may need to consider.

☙❧

"A SERVANT IS NOT GREATER THAN HIS MASTER; NOR IS HE WHO IS SENT GREATER THAN HE WHO SENT HIM."

John 13:16 NKJV

A JEALOUS GOD

Catherine heard all this, and quite out of countenance, could listen no longer. Amazed that Isabella could endure it, and jealous for her brother, she rose up, and saying she should join Mrs. Allen, proposed their walking. But for this Isabella showed no inclination. She was so amazingly tired, and it was so odious to parade about the pump-room; and if she moved from her seat she should miss her sisters; she was expecting her sisters every moment; so that her dearest Catherine must excuse her, and must sit quietly down again. But Catherine could be stubborn too; and Mrs. Allen just then coming up to propose their returning home, she joined her and walked out of the pump-room, leaving Isabella still sitting with Captain Tilney. With much uneasiness did she thus leave them. It seemed to her that Captain Tilney was falling in love with Isabella, and Isabella unconsciously encouraging him; unconsciously it must be, for Isabella's attachment to James was as certain and well acknowledged as her engagement. To doubt her truth or good intentions was impossible; and yet, during the whole of their conversation her manner had been odd. She wished Isabella had talked more like her usual self, and not so much about money, and had not looked so well pleased at the sight of Captain Tilney. How strange that she should not perceive his admiration! Catherine longed to give her a hint of it, to put her on her guard, and prevent all the pain which her too lively behaviour might otherwise create both for him and her brother.

—*Northanger Abbey*

Isabella's latest show of foolishness—recklessly flirting with Captain Tilney, when she is engaged to marry James—is inexcusable. Catherine, "jealous for her brother," leaves the party heartsick.

In this context, the word *jealous* represents a virtuous kind of jealousy—not the negative expression born of self-love and associated with fear and covetousness. We see this same virtuous jealousy referred to multiple times in Scripture—it is even used to name God. It is important to understand that this jealousy is not sinful; it *cannot* be, because it describes the Creator who knows no sin, whose loyalty to us is boundless and unending.

In 2 Corinthians 11, Paul wrote, "For I am jealous for you with godly jealousy. For I have betrothed you to one husband, that I may present you as a chaste virgin to Christ" (v. 2 NKJV). Paul was urging the Corinthians to forsake the idols and other gods in their lives, and to return to their "one husband," God. Paul's jealousy for the Corinthians is a picture of the same kind of love that the Father has for us. It is the same idea of a desire for Isabella's faithfulness that Catherine wishes for her brother James.

Like Isabella, we betray God, our Lover, when we flirt with foolish things and let them distract us from our purpose of serving and knowing the one true God. We can think of it as His desire to hold on to us, an unwillingness to let go no matter where or why our hearts wander. It is a protection, a gift from a sinless God.

❦

YOU SHALL WORSHIP NO OTHER GOD, FOR THE LORD,
WHOSE NAME IS JEALOUS, IS A JEALOUS GOD.

Exodus 34:14

GETTING ANGRY, YET NOT SINNING

"How very ill Eliza Bennet looks this morning, Mr. Darcy," she cried; "I never in my life saw any one so much altered as she is since the winter. She is grown so brown and coarse! Louisa and I were agreeing that we should not have known her again."

However little Mr. Darcy might have liked such an address, he contented himself with coolly replying that he perceived no other alteration than her being rather tanned—no miraculous consequence of travelling in the summer.

"For my own part," she rejoined, "I must confess that I never could see any beauty in her. Her face is too thin; her complexion has no brilliancy; and her features are not at all handsome. Her nose wants character; there is nothing marked in its lines. Her teeth are tolerable, but not out of the common way; and as for her eyes, which have sometimes been called so fine, I never could perceive any thing extraordinary in them. They have a sharp, shrewish look, which I do not like at all; and in her air altogether, there is a self-sufficiency without fashion which is intolerable."

Persuaded as Miss Bingley was that Darcy admired Elizabeth, this was not the best method of recommending herself; but angry people are not always wise.

—Pride and Prejudice

Miss Bingley is not only angry but also desperate— a dangerous combination. Were she a woman of self-control, she might be able to curb this. But she is instead given to self-indulgence, and the result is a barrage of unkind remarks about Elizabeth.

The reality is that daily, each of us encounters circumstances that raise our ire. No one is immune to anger—not even the most self-disciplined or most laid-back people. As Christians, we have to learn to halt the progress of anger in our lives before it turns into sin.

There is an interesting commentary on anger found in two juxtaposed verses in Ephesians 4: "Be angry and do not sin" (v. 26). Yet five verses later we read, "Let all bitterness and wrath and anger and clamor and slander be put away from you, along with all malice" (v. 31). Does this sound contradictory? In the first example we're being *told* it's okay to be angry, as long as we don't sin; in verse 31, we're instructed to put anger away from us. Which is it?

In order to understand the underlying message, we need to recognize that there are two kinds of anger. Verse 26 refers to the righteous anger of God; verse 31, to the manifestation of our flesh, which must be submitted to God's authority. This reveals something important: there is a kind of anger that is acceptable. In other words, there are things that *ought* to make us angry—injustice, immorality, indecency. Rest assured these things make God angry too!

But the second, and far more common, kind of anger is the one we have to deliberately choose to put off: sinful anger centered in self. Anything that gives the devil his opportunity must be stopped at the source. The only way to do this, of course, is to be constantly seeking and submitting ourselves to God.

The only way to clear your heart of offenses and grudges is to submit everything to the Lord in prayer. He can transform your thinking and help you experience the glory of freedom.

❦

GOOD SENSE MAKES ONE SLOW TO ANGER,
AND IT IS HIS GLORY TO OVERLOOK AN OFFENSE.

Proverbs 19:11

OBSESSING

In her earnest meditations on the contents of the letter . . . Elinor forgot the immediate distress of her sister, forgot that she had three letters on her lap yet unread, and so entirely forgot how long she had been in the room, that when on hearing a carriage drive up to the door, she went to the window to see who could be coming so unreasonably early, she was all astonishment to perceive Mrs. Jennings's chariot, which she knew had not been ordered till one.

Determined not to quit Marianne, though hopeless of contributing, at present, to her ease, she hurried away to excuse herself from attending Mrs. Jennings, on account of her sister being indisposed. Mrs. Jennings, with a thoroughly good-humoured concern for its cause, admitted the excuse most readily, and Elinor, after seeing her safe off, returned to Marianne, whom she found attempting to rise from the bed, and whom she reached just in time to prevent her from falling on the floor, faint and giddy from a long want of proper rest and food; for it was many days since she had any appetite, and many nights since she had really slept; and now, when her mind was no longer supported by the fever of suspense, the consequence of all this was felt in an aching head, a weakened stomach, and a general nervous faintness.

—Sense and Sensibility

The long-sought explanation for Willoughby's non-appearance in London has reached its conclusion: his letter to Marianne, which affirms his detachment in a chilling way, confirms his role as villain.

But is Marianne blameless? Unequivocally, no. Her unhealthy obsession with Willoughby went unchecked by any emotional or moral boundaries; it chased away her desire to care for even her health and kept her anchored in a "fever of suspense." Her fervor grew into an unhealthy mind-set, and now she is alone in her rejection.

Though a headstrong romantic like Marianne might argue that true love is worth the fall, the majority of us can attest to the wisdom in tempering obsession with equal measures of propriety and common sense.

As Christians, we carry an additional responsibility for checking our hearts against unhealthy obsessions: the very real threat of letting anything—even a good thing—preoccupy us to the point that it overshadows our relationship with the Lord.

Idolatry has always plagued mankind. Throughout the Old Testament, time and time again we see the nation of Israel stray from the one living God and set up false idols to worship. God even tells His people explicitly, in Exodus 20:3, "Thou shalt have no other gods before me" (KJV). Then He goes on to say, "For I the LORD your God am a jealous God" (v. 5).

Think about a good focus in your life that easily runs to obsession—your bank account, your reputation, your children (especially if one is rebelling), even your involvement in the church. Remember, anything that diverts your time or attention from the one true living God is in competition with Him. *He is a jealous God!*

Are you focused to an unhealthy degree on another person? Are you worshiping an activity or a possession that is hindering you from pure relationship with the Lord? Whatever the idols in your life, they need to be dethroned.

❦

THEIR SORROWS SHALL BE MULTIPLIED THAT HASTEN
AFTER ANOTHER GOD.

Psalm 16:4 KJV

A Changed Man

Sir Thomas was at that moment looking round him, and saying, "But where is Fanny? Why do not I see my little Fanny?"—and on perceiving her, came forward with a kindness which astonished and penetrated her, calling her his dear Fanny, kissing her affectionately, and observing with decided pleasure how much she was grown! Fanny knew not how to feel, nor where to look. She was quite oppressed. He had never been so kind, so very kind to her in his life. His manner seemed changed, his voice was quick from the agitation of joy; and all that had been awful in his dignity seemed lost in tenderness. He led her nearer the light and looked at her again—inquired particularly after her health, and then, correcting himself, observed that he need not inquire, for her appearance spoke sufficiently on that point.

A fine blush having succeeded the previous paleness of her face, he was justified in his belief of her equal improvement in health and beauty. He inquired next after her family, especially William: and his kindness altogether was such as made her reproach herself for loving him so little, and thinking his return a misfortune; and when, on having courage to lift her eyes to his face, she saw that he was grown thinner, and had the burnt, fagged, worn look of fatigue and a hot climate, every tender feeling was increased, and she was miserable in considering how much unsuspected vexation was probably ready to burst on him.

—*Mansfield Park*

S ir Thomas Bertram has returned home from the West Indies a changed man. To Fanny, whose previous encounters with her gruff uncle caused her to dread his return, Sir Thomas's overwhelming kindness is a welcome change.

The apostle Paul underwent an even more radical change. Formerly known as Saul, a highly educated Roman Jew who persecuted Christians, Paul was stopped by God on the road to Damascus. Ironically, God had to blind Paul (temporarily) before Paul could see clearly: "Suddenly a light from heaven flashed around him. . . . Saul rose from the ground, and although his eyes were opened, he saw nothing. So they led him by the hand and brought him into Damascus. And for three days he was without sight, and neither ate nor drank" (Acts 9:3, 8–9). After that encounter, the singular focus of Paul's life became spreading the gospel.

Because of the radical nature of his conversion, Paul was able to identify with other nonbelievers. In 2 Corinthians, Paul wrote, "The god of this age has blinded the minds of unbelievers, so that they cannot see the light of the gospel of the glory of Christ, who is the image of God" (4:4 NIV). Paul understood that spiritual blindness is a condition we need deliverance from.

If your life needs changing, pray that God would open the eyes of your heart. He is the only one capable of such transformation.

❦

I DO NOT CEASE TO GIVE THANKS FOR YOU, . . . THAT THE
GOD OF OUR LORD JESUS CHRIST . . . MAY GIVE YOU A
SPIRIT OF WISDOM AND OF REVELATION IN THE KNOWLEDGE
OF HIM, HAVING THE EYES OF YOUR HEARTS ENLIGHTENED.

Ephesians 1:16–18

God's Rules Are for Our Protection

If gratitude and esteem are good foundations of affection, Elizabeth's change of sentiment will be neither improbable nor faulty. But if otherwise, if the regard springing from such sources is unreasonable or unnatural, in comparison of what is so often described as arising on a first interview with its object, and even before two words have been exchanged, nothing can be said in her defence, except that she had given somewhat of a trial to the latter method in her partiality for Wickham, and that its ill-success might perhaps authorise her to seek the other less interesting mode of attachment. Be that as it may, she saw him go with regret; and in this early example of what Lydia's infamy must produce, found additional anguish as she reflected on that wretched business. Never, since reading Jane's second letter, had she entertained a hope of Wickham's meaning to marry her. No one but Jane, she thought, could flatter herself with such an expectation. Surprise was the least of her feelings on this developement. While the contents of the first letter remained on her mind, she was all surprise—all astonishment that Wickham should marry a girl whom it was impossible he could marry for money; and how Lydia could ever have attached him had appeared incomprehensible. But now it was all too natural. For such an attachment as this, she might have sufficient charms; and though she did not suppose Lydia to be deliberately engaging in an elopement, without the intention of marriage, she had no difficulty in believing that neither her virtue nor her understanding would preserve her from falling an easy prey.

—Pride and Prejudice

After receiving Jane's two letters, Elizabeth is sick with dismay. Not only has her thoughtless sister Lydia run away with Mr. Wickham; but it appears they are not married yet, and that Mr. Wickham has no intention of going through with it. In Jane Austen's day, this type of breach in etiquette would usher in nearly unheard-of disgrace: not only would it ruin Lydia's reputation for life, but also the reputation of the entire Bennet family.

Viewed through a modern-day lens, the gravity of this circumstance reads more like a situational comedy. Statistics show that more couples live together before marriage than ever. Given its widespread acceptance, it has become unfashionable to call cohabitation by its real name: sin. But according to God's laws, it is just that.

In order to understand *why* cohabitation is sin, we first have to recognize that sin is *anything that goes against the nature of God*. First Thessalonians 5:22–23 says, "Abstain from all appearance of evil. And the very God of peace sanctify you wholly; and I pray God your whole spirit and soul and body be preserved blameless unto the coming of our Lord Jesus Christ" (KJV). As Christians, the goal we should have in every relationship is to honor the Lord and make His name known. The choice to live together without the God-blessed benefit of marriage prioritizes selfishness over God.

God gave us His laws in the Bible for our good—to safeguard us. They aren't meant to deny us pleasure or fun, but to steer us into relationships that can ultimately glorify Him.

❧

DIDN'T YOU REALIZE THAT YOUR BODY IS A SACRED PLACE,
THE PLACE OF THE HOLY SPIRIT? DON'T YOU SEE THAT
YOU CAN'T LIVE HOWEVER YOU PLEASE, SQUANDERING
WHAT GOD PAID SUCH A HIGH PRICE FOR?

1 Corinthians 6:19 MSG

IDLE GOSSIP

The rest of the dinner passed away; the dessert succeeded, the children came in, and were talked to and admired amid the usual rate of conversation; a few clever things said, a few downright silly, but by much the larger proportion neither the one nor the other—nothing worse than everyday remarks, dull repetitions, old news, and heavy jokes.

The ladies had not been long in the drawing-room, before the other ladies, in their different divisions, arrived. Emma watched the entree of her own particular little friend; and if she could not exult in her dignity and grace, she could not only love the blooming sweetness and the artless manner, but could most heartily rejoice in that light, cheerful, unsentimental disposition which allowed her so many alleviations of pleasure, in the midst of the pangs of disappointed affection. There she sat—and who would have guessed how many tears she had been lately shedding? To be in company, nicely dressed herself and seeing others nicely dressed, to sit and smile and look pretty, and say nothing, was enough for the happiness of the present hour. Jane Fairfax did look and move superior; but Emma suspected she might have been glad to change feelings with Harriet, very glad to have purchased the mortification of having loved—yes, of having loved even Mr. Elton in vain—by the surrender of all the dangerous pleasure of knowing herself beloved by the husband of her friend.

—*Emma*

One of the dangers of living a life of creature comforts is that it encourages idle speculation about the secret lives of others. It is a tendency perfectly encapsulated in this after-dinner party scene, where Emma watches Harriet and Jane Fairfax and imagines that she knows exactly what is going on in their personal lives.

Of course it is important to demonstrate concern and empathy for others, and in one sense that is Emma's intent. But when a young woman with both time and resources lacks important mental and spiritual disciplines in her life, simple observations can quickly grow into idle speculation.

Left unchecked, speculation opens the door to feelings like judgment, jealousy, and slander. Paul addressed this when he wrote, "[Young unmarried women] . . . learn to be idlers, going about from house to house, and not only idlers, but also gossips and busybodies, saying what they should not" (1 Timothy 5:13). His words are written specifically about young unmarried widows, but they apply equally to unmarried *and* married women—and are certainly applicable to a certain young protagonist who is determined never to marry.

When you find yourself with close friends, do you "share" more information than necessary about another friend? Does your thought life sometimes lead to speculating about things that do nothing to develop your own character or build up those around you? Think about how you would want to be thought of, spoken about, and treated—and strive to emulate that example.

ॐ

"JUDGE NOT, THAT YOU BE NOT JUDGED. FOR WITH THE
JUDGMENT YOU PRONOUNCE YOU WILL BE JUDGED, AND WITH
THE MEASURE YOU USE IT WILL BE MEASURED TO YOU."

Matthew 7:1–2

SILLINESS

[Catherine's] greedy eye glanced rapidly over a page. She started at its import. Could it be possible, or did not her senses play her false? An inventory of linen, in coarse and modern characters, seemed all that was before her! If the evidence of sight might be trusted, she held a washing-bill in her hand. She seized another sheet, and saw the same articles with little variation; a third, a fourth, and a fifth presented nothing new. Shirts, stockings, cravats, and waistcoats faced her in each. Two others, penned by the same hand, marked an expenditure scarcely more interesting, in letters, hair-powder, shoe-string, and breeches-ball. And the larger sheet, which had enclosed the rest, seemed by its first cramp line, "To poultice chestnut mare"—a farrier's bill! Such was the collection of papers (left perhaps, as she could then suppose, by the negligence of a servant in the place whence she had taken them) which had filled her with expectation and alarm, and robbed her of half her night's rest! She felt humbled to the dust. Could not the adventure of the chest have taught her wisdom? A corner of it, catching her eye as she lay, seemed to rise up in judgment against her. Nothing could now be clearer than the absurdity of her recent fancies. To suppose that a manuscript of many generations back could have remained undiscovered in a room such as that, so modern, so habitable!—Or that she should be the first to possess the skill of unlocking a cabinet, the key of which was open to all!

—Northanger Abbey

atherine's mind has feasted for years on Gothic novels like *The Mysteries of Udolpho*; small wonder, then, that she anticipates horror and mayhem around every corner at Northanger Abbey. But in the cold light of dawn, Catherine has met with a startling truth: the ream of papers that she imagined to contain a mysterious age-old manuscript is nothing more than a prosaic inventory of linens.

While Jane Austen is parodying the popular romantic novels of her time, there is also a morality lesson at play here: Catherine's God-given imagination has not been fed with spiritually nourishing food, but with vacuous popular novels and other forms of useless entertainment. The result is a young woman who has schooled herself in silliness and is ready to accept whatever she is told.

Today, the Gothic novel has been replaced by a combination of television, movies, music, romance novels, and a thousand other forms of entertainment that, given control in our lives, distract us from growing into mature Christians who can set an example for others. But in Hebrews we find the answer: "For the *word of God is living and active*, sharper than any two-edged sword, piercing to the division of soul and of spirit, of joints and of marrow, and discerning the thoughts and intentions of the heart" (4:12, emphasis added).

If they're to be profitable, our entertainment choices must be filtered through godly counsel and Scripture before they are given a place in our lives. Ask God to help you evaluate the things you choose to see, read, and hear. He gave you a wonderful imagination, but it's up to you to use it for His glory.

❧

BUT SOLID FOOD IS FOR THE MATURE, FOR THOSE WHO
HAVE THEIR POWERS OF DISCERNMENT TRAINED BY
CONSTANT PRACTICE TO DISTINGUISH GOOD FROM EVIL.

Hebrews 5:14

Speaking the Truth in Love

"But does Lydia know nothing of this? Can she be ignorant of what you and Jane seem so well to understand?"

"Oh, yes!—that, that is the worst of all. Till I was in Kent, and saw so much both of Mr. Darcy and his relation, Colonel Fitzwilliam, I was ignorant of the truth myself. And when I returned home, the —shire was to leave Meryton in a week or fortnight's time. As that was the case, neither Jane, to whom I related the whole, nor I, thought it necessary to make our knowledge public; for of what use could it apparently be to any one that the good opinion which all the neighbourhood had of him should then be overthrown? And even when it was settled that Lydia should go with Mrs. Forster, the necessity of opening her eyes to his character never occurred to me. That she could be in any danger from the deception never entered my head. That such a consequence as this should ensue, you may easily believe was far enough from my thoughts." . . .

It may be easily believed that, however little of novelty could be added to their fears, hopes, and conjectures, on this interesting subject by its repeated discussion, no other could detain them from it long, during the whole of the journey. From Elizabeth's thoughts it was never absent. Fixed there by the keenest of all anguish, self-reproach, she could find no interval of ease or forgetfulness.

—Pride and Prejudice

With the benefit of hindsight, Elizabeth desperately regrets her decision not to tell Lydia about Mr. Wickham. Now her sister's reputation is in peril, a fact for which Elizabeth cannot forgive herself: "Fixed there by the keenest of all anguish, self-reproach, she could find no interval of ease or forgetfulness."

This sequence of events proves that sometimes, it is best to speak the truth in love. The term comes from Ephesians 4:15, "Speaking the truth in love, we will in all things grow up into him who is the Head, that is, Christ" (NIV). This means proclaiming the truth boldly and completely—without watering it down, without holding back, but also treating the listener with compassion, as Christ would.

Elizabeth wasn't willing to risk offending her sister and perhaps damaging the relationship (now the relationship is damaged because she *didn't* speak the truth in love). One of the defining characteristics of living a sold-out Christian life is that we're willing to take that risk if it means helping a brother or sister.

Obviously, speaking the truth in love does not give us free license to hurt someone's feelings or spread gossip. In order to fulfill Christ's command, we must use godly wisdom and discernment concerning both *how* we approach others and *what* we say when we do. Remember that if your focus is on God, then any truth spoken in love—both given and received—will only facilitate the goal of unity in the body of Christ.

❦

YOU HAVE HEARD OF THIS HOPE BEFORE IN THE WORD
OF THE TRUTH, THE GOSPEL.

Colossians 1:5 NRSV

SEEING GOD IN NATURE

"This is pretty, very pretty," said Fanny, looking around her. . . .

Miss Crawford, untouched and inattentive, had nothing to say; and Fanny, perceiving it, brought back her own mind to what she thought must interest.

"It may seem impertinent in me to praise, but I must admire the taste Mrs. Grant has shewn in all this. There is such a quiet simplicity in the plan of the walk! Not too much attempted!"

"Yes," replied Miss Crawford carelessly, "it does very well for a place of this sort. One does not think of extent here; and between ourselves, till I came to Mansfield, I had not imagined a country parson ever aspired to a shrubbery, or anything of the kind."

"I am so glad to see the evergreens thrive!" said Fanny, in reply. "My uncle's gardener always says the soil here is better than his own, and so it appears from the growth of the laurels and evergreens in general. The evergreen! How beautiful, how welcome, how wonderful the evergreen! When one thinks of it, how astonishing a variety of nature! In some countries we know the tree that sheds its leaf is the variety, but that does not make it less amazing that the same soil and the same sun should nurture plants differing in the first rule and law of their existence. You will think me rhapsodising; but when I am out of doors, especially when I am sitting out of doors, I am very apt to get into this sort of wondering strain. One cannot fix one's eyes on the commonest natural production without finding food for a rambling fancy."

—*Mansfield Park*

On a visit with Mary Crawford, Fanny cannot help but admire the lovely grounds of the parsonage. Mary, whose idea of beauty does not extend to country life, finds Fanny's dialogue tiresome; but the country girl in Fanny knows of nothing more beautiful than the trees and fields stretching out before them. Because Fanny takes so much pleasure in the natural world, she can't see "the commonest natural production without finding food for a rambling fancy." She is a true appreciator of nature.

Creation is a vivid expression of God's nature. Those who appreciate it, as Fanny does, are quick to exclaim their admiration of it. It is why we are moved by a beautiful sunset, a towering mountain, or a raging river: we can't be silent in the face of such magnificent beauty!

Indeed, natural beauty is one of the most personal, intimate ways God reveals His character to us. Isn't that enough to make you rejoice? The psalmist was rejoicing when he wrote the words, "I lift up my eyes to the hills. From where does my help come? My help comes from the LORD, who made heaven and earth" (Psalm 121:1–2).

When you look out at creation, remember God's greatness. The same God who created breathtaking vistas and towering precipices is the God who comforts you in moments of weakness . . . who thought of you before you were born . . . who offered His Son's life in exchange for yours. Consider His splendor, and rejoice!

❧

THE HEAVENS DECLARE THE GLORY OF GOD,
AND THE SKY ABOVE PROCLAIMS HIS HANDIWORK.

Psalm 19:1

RISING ABOVE

About this time the two Miss Steeles, lately arrived at their cousin's house in Bartlett's Buildings, Holburn, presented themselves again before their more grand relations in Conduit and Berkeley Streets; and were welcomed by them all with great cordiality.

Elinor only was sorry to see them. Their presence always gave her pain, and she hardly knew how to make a very gracious return to the overpowering delight of Lucy in finding her still in town.

"I should have been quite disappointed if I had not found you here still," said she repeatedly, with a strong emphasis on the word. "But I always thought I should. I was almost sure you would not leave London yet awhile; though you told me, you know, at Barton, that you should not stay above a month. But I thought, at the time, that you would most likely change your mind when it came to the point. It would have been such a great pity to have went away before your brother and sister came. And now to be sure you will be in no hurry to be gone. I am amazingly glad you did not keep to your word."

Elinor perfectly understood her, and was forced to use all her self-command to make it appear that she did not.

—Sense and Sensibility

This humorous scene further exposes Lucy Steele's character as manipulative and self-serving—exactly what we have come to expect. As antagonists go, Lucy is an easy target for dislike: she is sneaky, double-tongued, and seems intent on breaking poor Elinor's heart. In moments like these, a character this wretched gets our full disapproval.

What's admirable in this scene—and countless others like it—is how successfully Elinor uses self-command to hold back a sharp retort. With this action, she demonstrates how one successfully stops an aggressor like Lucy: by refusing to stoop to her level.

This was not only the height of good manners in eighteen-century England; it is also the way Christ instructs us to respond to those who mistreat or speak ill of us. In Matthew 5.39, He tells the crowd gathered to listen to His Sermon on the Mount, "But I tell you, Do not resist an evil person. If someone strikes you on the right cheek, turn to him the other also" (NIV).

It is no secret that Elinor neither likes nor trusts Lucy (and with good reason!), but her sense of diplomacy keeps her from stooping to Lucy's level. Whether Jane Austen's motivation in crafting this plot device was born of good manners or a desire to please the Lord, we do not know. Regardless, it is fitting that a character like Elinor should be upheld as a model of Christian behavior.

We will all encounter a Lucy Steele at some point in life. The important thing is to be prepared. How will you handle the next barbed comment or veiled criticism? Pray about what it means in your life to "turn the other cheek," and resolve to do it. It won't be easy. But by taking the high road, you will extinguish the spark Satan is trying to fan into a flame.

❦

WHERE NO WOOD IS, THERE THE FIRE GOETH OUT:
SO WHERE THERE IS NO TALEBEARER, THE STRIFE CEASETH.

Proverbs 26:20 KJV

CHOOSING IDOLS OVER GOD

MY DEAR [Mr. Bennet],

I feel myself called upon by our relationship, and my situation in life, to condole with you on the grievous affliction you are now suffering under, of which we were yesterday informed by a letter from Hertfordshire. . . .

The death of your daughter would have been a blessing in comparison of this. And it is the more to be lamented, because there is reason to suppose, as my dear Charlotte informs me, that this licentiousness of behaviour in your daughter has proceeded from a faulty degree of indulgence, though at the same time, for the consolation of yourself and Mrs. Bennet, I am inclined to think that her own disposition must be naturally bad, or she could not be guilty of such an enormity at so early an age. Howsoever that may be, you are grievously to be pitied, in which opinion I am not only joined by Mrs. Collins, but likewise by Lady Catherine and her daughter, to whom I have related the affair. They agree with me in apprehending that this false step in one daughter will be injurious to the fortunes of all the others; for who, as Lady Catherine herself condescendingly says, will connect themselves with such a family. And this consideration leads me moreover to reflect with augmented satisfaction on a certain event of last November, for had it been otherwise, I must have been involved in all your sorrow and disgrace. Let me advise you then, my dear Sir, to console yourself as much as possible, to throw off your unworthy child from your affection for ever, and leave her to reap the fruits of her own heinous offence.

—Pride and Prejudice

Laced through with insufferable sentiments— "licentiousness of behaviour," "faulty degree of indulgence," "sorrow and disgrace," and "her own disposition must be naturally bad"—Mr. Collins's letter to Mr. Bennet is like salt in an already festering wound: "Throw off your unworthy child from your affection for ever, and leave her to reap the fruits of her own heinous offence." Mr. Collins is urging the Bennets to save the reputation of their remaining daughters by disowning Lydia. According to some literary critics, if Wickham were to have abandoned Lydia, it would likely have led to her becoming a prostitute in London—an all-too-common fate for a disgraced woman with no resources.

In the book of Hosea, God uses a prostitute named Gomer to represent the sinful nation of Israel. Gomer's repeated unfaithfulness to her husband, the prophet Hosea, illustrates how the Israelites turned their backs on God to worship idols. The picture of God's abundant mercy throughout Hosea is breathtaking: "I will sow her for myself in the land. And I will have mercy on No Mercy, and I will say to Not My People, 'You are my people'; and he shall say, 'You are my God'" (2:23).

Like Gomer, we too forget how much He loves us, from how much He has saved us, and how much we hurt Him by choosing to worship other things. We also see that despite all this, He pursues us, and through repentance we are saved from eternal separation.

Consider just how much our sinful mistakes really cost Him, and yet He continues to pursue us with His grace and mercy. Now, that is a Love worth remembering.

❧

As indeed he says in Hosea, "Those who were not
my people I will call 'my people,' and her who was
not beloved I will call 'beloved.'"

Romans 9:25

A Bright Outlook

In the course of a second visit, [Mrs. Smith] talked with great openness, and Anne's astonishment increased. She could scarcely imagine a more cheerless situation in itself than Mrs Smith's. She had been very fond of her husband: she had buried him. She had been used to affluence: it was gone. She had no child to connect her with life and happiness again, no relations to assist in the arrangement of perplexed affairs, no health to make all the rest supportable. Her accommodations were limited to a noisy parlour, and a dark bedroom behind, with no possibility of moving from one to the other without assistance, which there was only one servant in the house to afford, and she never quitted the house but to be conveyed into the warm bath. Yet, in spite of all this, Anne had reason to believe that she had moments only of languor and depression, to hours of occupation and enjoyment. How could it be? She watched, observed, reflected, and finally determined that this was not a case of fortitude or of resignation only. A submissive spirit might be patient, a strong understanding would supply resolution, but here was something more; here was that elasticity of mind, that disposition to be comforted, that power of turning readily from evil to good, and of finding employment which carried her out of herself, which was from nature alone. It was the choicest gift of Heaven; and Anne viewed her friend as one of those instances in which, by a merciful appointment, it seems designed to counterbalance almost every other want.

—Persuasion

Anne's old friend Mrs. Smith is one of Jane Austen's few truly impoverished characters—a crippled widow who is physically and financially destitute following a series of unfortunate circumstances. Yet her countenance remains cheerful and generous! Upon close observation, Anne concludes that her friend's temperament is the "choicest gift of Heaven"—another way of saying that Mrs. Smith has been blessed by God with her optimistic outlook. Anne deems it a quality that compensates for every other thing that is lacking in her life.

No matter what our circumstances, you and I have a God-given reason to rejoice too: "And we know that God causes everything to work together for the good of those who love God and are called according to his purpose for them" (Romans 8:28 NLT). The God of the universe, who spoke everything into being and who created each of us, has called us to Himself. We are given purpose through our identification as His sons and daughters; we know that God is in control. Our primary job is to trust, believe, and follow Him closely, even when life does not feel rewarding, pleasant, or productive. Thanks to the nature and the character of God, growing closer and closer to Him will produce the natural response of worship.

Look for ways in your life to express joy and thankfulness, even amid trials; determine not to get bogged down by your present situation. God chooses to love us; we can, in turn, choose to be grateful with our hearts and our lips. Remember, we are *saved for eternity*. That is reason enough to rejoice!

❦

YOUR ATTITUDE SHOULD BE THE SAME AS THAT OF
CHRIST JESUS.

Philippians 2.5 NIV

When God's Favor Doesn't Look Like Favor

[*Mrs. Norris to Fanny:*] *"The nonsense and folly of people's stepping out of their rank and trying to appear above themselves, makes me think it right to give you a hint, Fanny, now that you are going into company without any of us; and I do beseech and entreat you not to be putting yourself forward, and talking and giving your opinion as if you were one of your cousins—as if you were dear Mrs. Rushworth or Julia. That will never do, believe me. Remember, wherever you are, you must be the lowest and last; and though Miss Crawford is in a manner at home at the Parsonage, you are not to be taking place of her. And as to coming away at night, you are to stay just as long as Edmund chuses. Leave him to settle that."*

"Yes, ma'am, I should not think of anything else."

"And if it should rain, which I think exceedingly likely, for I never saw it more threatening for a wet evening in my life, you must manage as well as you can, and not be expecting the carriage to be sent for you. I certainly do not go home to-night, and, therefore, the carriage will not be out on my account; so you must make up your mind to what may happen, and take your things accordingly."

Her niece thought it perfectly reasonable. She rated her own claims to comfort as low even as Mrs. Norris could.

—Mansfield Park

Like a schoolyard bully, Mrs. Norris never misses an opportunity to remind Fanny how lucky she is to live at Mansfield, how inferior she is to her cousins, and that she must be "lowest and last." Surprisingly, Aunt Norris's treatment serves a valuable purpose: it reminds Fanny to forgive, to extend grace, and to appreciate those who love her unconditionally—Edmund and William. In a roundabout way, this bitter pill of an aunt is teaching Fanny to become more like Jesus.

The Bible's Joseph endured unjust treatment too—from enslavement at the hands of his brothers to wrongful imprisonment for resisting advances from Potiphar's wife. Yet the Bible makes clear that a thread of favor is woven through Joseph's life as we read again and again, *"But the LORD was with Joseph and showed him steadfast love and gave him favor"* (Genesis 39:21, emphasis added). Granted, Joseph had to look hard to see the favor beneath the bitter pill of his circumstances—and he did. Without wavering, he chose to believe in God's steadfast love and to remember that God had a plan for his life.

Do you believe that God has a plan and a purpose for your life, even when you're frustrated by circumstances or people? Like Joseph and Fanny, choose to take the high road: refuse to nurse resentment and instead extend forgiveness and choose to trust in the One who is ultimately in control. *Know* that God is faithful, and look hard to see His thread of favor in your life—you'll find it.

❧

BE HUMBLE, THINKING OF OTHERS AS BETTER THAN YOURSELF. DON'T JUST THINK ABOUT YOUR OWN AFFAIRS, BUT BE INTERESTED IN OTHERS, TOO, AND IN WHAT THEY ARE DOING.

Philippians 2:3–4 TLB

Mr. Gardiner did not write again till he had received an answer from Colonel Forster; and then he had nothing of a pleasant nature to send. It was not known that Wickham had a single relation with whom he kept up any connection, and it was certain that he had no near one living. His former acquaintance had been numerous; but since he had been in the militia, it did not appear that he was on terms of particular friendship with any of them. There was no one therefore who could be pointed out as likely to give any news of him. And in the wretched state of his own finances there was a very powerful motive for secrecy, in addition to his fear of discovery by Lydia's relations, for it had just transpired that he had left gaming debts behind him, to a very considerable amount. Colonel Forster believed that more than a thousand pounds would be necessary to clear his expences at Brighton. He owed a good deal in the town, but his debts of honour were still more for-midable. Mr. Gardiner did not attempt to conceal these particulars from the Longbourn family; Jane heard them with horror. "A gamester!" she cried. "This is wholly unexpected. I had not an idea of it."

—Pride and Prejudice

The news that Wickham left town deeply in debt is sobering: in Jane Austen's day, any gentleman would not rack up debts and leave them unpaid. We have already seen evidence that Mr. Wickham is driven by the pursuit of money, in that he gambled away the fortune left to him by the elder Mr. Darcy, pursued young women like Miss King and Miss Darcy for their dowries, and now has run away with Lydia in an apparent effort to extort money from her family. Wherever he travels Wickham accrues debt, both emotional and monetary.

Interestingly, through his interaction with Wickham, Mr. Darcy is gradually revealed as a hero figure. He clears Wickham (and Lydia, by extension) by paying off his outstanding credit and canceling the debt. Though Wickham may not appreciate the kindness, it does not go unnoticed by Elizabeth.

We criticize Wickham's selfishness, but how easily you and I forget about our own debt. God in the beginning created us to love and honor Him; every time we sin, we rack up spiritual debt. Thankfully, we have a Redeemer who willingly acted as mediator and paid the ransom. This is what Jesus was referring to when He prayed, "Forgive us our debts, as we also have forgiven our debtors" (Matthew 6:12). Through His sinless life and substitutionary death, Jesus cleared our names and freed us to live new lives, resulting in an eternal inheritance!

Think how much you have been forgiven, the sacrifice made on your behalf. And the next time you start to hold a grudge or add up how much someone owes you, remember that the price for your life—now and eternal—has been paid; you are gloriously free to extend grace to others.

⚬❦⚬

"FOR EVEN THE SON OF MAN DID NOT COME TO BE
SERVED BUT TO SERVE, AND TO GIVE HIS LIFE AS A
RANSOM FOR MANY."

Mark 10:45

FORGIVENESS

The idea of wanting gratitude and consideration for Miss Woodhouse, whom she really loved extremely, made her wretched for a while, and when the violence of grief was comforted away, still remained powerful enough to prompt to what was right and support her in it very tolerably.

"You, who have been the best friend I ever had in my life—Want gratitude to you!—Nobody is equal to you!—I care for nobody as I do for you!—Oh! Miss Woodhouse, how ungrateful I have been!"

Such expressions, assisted as they were by every thing that look and manner could do, made Emma feel that she had never loved Harriet so well, nor valued her affection so highly before.

"There is no charm equal to tenderness of heart," said she afterwards to herself. "There is nothing to be compared to it. Warmth and tenderness of heart, with an affectionate, open manner, will beat all the clearness of head in the world, for attraction, I am sure it will. It is tenderness of heart which makes my dear father so generally beloved—which gives Isabella all her popularity.—I have it not—but I know how to prize and respect it.—Harriet is my superior in all the charm and all the felicity it gives. Dear Harriet!—I would not change you for the clearest-headed, longest-sighted, best-judging female breathing. Oh! the coldness of a Jane Fairfax!—Harriet is worth a hundred such—And for a wife—a sensible man's wife—it is invaluable. I mention no names; but happy the man who changes Emma for Harriet!"

—*Emma*

When Emma tearfully confesses to Harriet that she greatly misjudged Mr. Elton—that his affection lay with the former, and not the latter—she expected to meet with anger and reproach. Certainly she deserves Harriet's fury: Emma had meddled in her friend's love life with disastrous results. Instead, Harriet responds with forgiveness, warmth, and even gratitude.

How can Harriet pardon Emma so freely? Because she loves her. No questions asked, unconditionally.

It is the same with our heavenly Father. We hurt Him every time we sin, yet He generously paid the price of our forgiveness before we even asked. His loving example shows us the way we are meant to love and forgive each other—without conditions, no matter what the wrong.

If we struggle to forgive others, it only demonstrates that we have not truly experienced God's forgiveness ourselves. "For if you forgive others their trespasses, your heavenly Father will also forgive you, but if you do not forgive others their trespasses, neither will your Father forgive your trespasses" (Matthew 6:14–15). In other words, you must fully accept God's gift of forgiveness—through His Son's redemptive work on the cross—before you can extend it to others.

Is there someone against whom you are harboring a secret resentment? Are you withholding forgiveness because you haven't been asked? Think about all you've been forgiven of yourself, and rejoice in the example you are called to follow.

❧

IF WE CONFESS OUR SINS, HE IS FAITHFUL AND JUST TO
FORGIVE US OUR SINS AND TO CLEANSE US FROM ALL
UNRIGHTEOUSNESS.

1 John 1:9

NOT GETTING DISTRACTED

[Mr. Dashwood] paused for [Elinor's] assent and compassion; and she forced herself to say, "Your expenses both in town and country must certainly be considerable; but your income is a large one."

"Not so large, I dare say, as many people suppose. I do not mean to complain, however; it is undoubtedly a comfortable one, and I hope will in time be better. . . . Other great and inevitable expenses too we have had on first coming to Norland. Our respected father, as you well know, bequeathed all the Stanhill effects that remained at Norland (and very valuable they were) to your mother. Far be it from ME to repine at his doing so; he had an undoubted right to dispose of his own property as he chose, but, in consequence of it, we have been obliged to make large purchases of linen, china, &c. to supply the place of what was taken away. You may guess, after all these expenses, how very far we must be from being rich, and how acceptable Mrs. Ferrars's kindness is."

"Certainly," said Elinor; "and assisted by her liberality, I hope you may yet live to be in easy circumstances."

"Another year or two may do much towards it," he gravely replied; "but however there is still a great deal to be done."

Having now said enough to make his poverty clear, and to do away the necessity of buying a pair of ear-rings for each of his sisters, in his next visit at Gray's his thoughts took a cheerfuller turn.

—*Sense and Sensibility*

Mr. John Dashwood has three serious faults: he is easily swayed by his manipulative shrew of a wife, Fanny; his selfish decisions render his father's widow and three daughters nearly impoverished; and his conscience about all this is *just* sensitive enough that he scrambles to absolve himself frequently. He does so using the most preposterous method: by attempting to convince Elinor (and whomever else will listen) that he is on the verge of financial bankruptcy.

Elinor is not fooled. But to her credit, nor does she choose to judge her brother. This is perhaps the key to living in a world of hypocrites: she does not let it *bother* her. One might argue that she has a great deal more on her mind than John Dashwood's weak character. But it's equally conceivable that Elinor has learned to retain what is important and shed that which is not. John Dashwood's lengthy case for his own near poverty clearly fits into the latter category.

The writer of Proverbs summarized this phenomenon: "A gracious woman attains honor, and ruthless men attain riches" (11:16 NASB). To put it another way, a gracious woman enjoys favor and acceptance in God's sight; a ruthless man stockpiles material wealth, which does nothing for the state of his soul. For all of John's material wealth, his character falls short of Elinor's in every way.

Whether you value grace or riches most in life is best reflected in how you spend your time. Seek to build your character over your bank account, and you will find God's blessing revealed in numerous unexpected ways.

❧

"FOR WHAT DOES IT PROFIT A MAN TO GAIN THE
WHOLE WORLD AND FORFEIT HIS SOUL?"

Mark 8:36

LIVING BY GRACE

[Mr. Darcy:] "What did you say of me, that I did not deserve? For, though your accusations were ill-founded, formed on mistaken premises, my behaviour to you at the time had merited the severest reproof. It was unpardonable. I cannot think of it without abhorrence."

"We will not quarrel for the greater share of blame annexed to that evening," said Elizabeth. "The conduct of neither, if strictly examined, will be irreproachable; but since then, we have both, I hope, improved in civility."

"I cannot be so easily reconciled to myself. The recollection of what I then said, of my conduct, my manners, my expressions during the whole of it, is now, and has been many months, inexpressibly painful to me. Your reproof, so well applied, I shall never forget: 'had you behaved in a more gentleman-like manner.' Those were your words. You know not, you can scarcely conceive, how they have tortured me;—though it was some time, I confess, before I was reasonable enough to allow their justice."

"I was certainly very far from expecting them to make so strong an impression. I had not the smallest idea of their being ever felt in such a way."

"I can easily believe it. You thought me then devoid of every proper feeling, I am sure you did. The turn of your countenance I shall never forget, as you said that I could not have addressed you in any possible way that would induce you to accept me."

"Oh! do not repeat what I then said. These recollections will not do at all. I assure you that I have long been most heartily ashamed of it."

—Pride and Prejudice

Now fully in love, Elizabeth and Darcy are freely and profusely apologizing for their early treatment of each other. Both are embarrassed by how ridiculously they spoke, and they willingly make a list of their personal deficiencies. Assuming they continue to seek mutual repentance, forgiveness, and grace, their future as a couple will be long and fruitful.

Darcy and Elizabeth's eloquent exchange offers a sweet picture of the forgiveness we receive when we come to Christ. We see our own sin—both toward Him and others—and are ashamed of our inadequacies. Through confession, we glimpse His overwhelming grace in His loving pursuit of us. We rejoice that He forgives us and calls us His own!

Unfortunately, because we live in a fallen world, we continue to confront circumstances that expose us to pain, grief, anger, and frustration. If we don't consistently and deliberately empty ourselves of pride and confess our sins to God and one another, seeds of bitterness may take root. Left untended, they hold the potential to choke out God's joy in our lives. Hebrews 12:15 says, "See to it that no one misses the grace of God and that no bitter root grows up to cause trouble and defile many" (NIV).

We are the benefactors of His grace, but we have to work at humbling our hearts and communicating openly with Him. Only then can we extend the same magnificent grace to others.

❦

BE KIND TO EACH OTHER, TENDERHEARTED,
FORGIVING ONE ANOTHER, JUST AS GOD THROUGH
CHRIST HAS FORGIVEN YOU.

Ephesians 4:32 NLT

BEWARE OF VIPERS

And without attempting any farther remonstrance, [Mary] left Fanny to her fate, a fate which, had not Fanny's heart been guarded in a way unsuspected by Miss Crawford, might have been a little harder than she deserved; for although there doubtless are such unconquerable young ladies of eighteen (or one should not read about them) as are never to be persuaded into love against their judgment by all that talent, manner, attention, and flattery can do, I have no inclination to believe Fanny one of them, or to think that with so much tenderness of disposition, and so much taste as belonged to her, she could have escaped heart-whole from the courtship (though the courtship only of a fortnight) of such a man as [Henry] Crawford, in spite of there being some previous ill opinion of him to be overcome, had not her affection been engaged elsewhere. With all the security which love of another and disesteem of him could give to the peace of mind he was attacking, his continued attentions—continued, but not obtrusive, and adapting themselves more and more to the gentleness and delicacy of her character—obliged her very soon to dislike him less than formerly. She had by no means forgotten the past, and she thought as ill of him as ever; but she felt his powers: he was entertaining; and his manners were so improved, so polite, so seriously and blamelessly polite, that it was impossible not to be civil to him in return.

—*Mansfield Park*

In this scene we see the well-laid trap Henry is setting for Fanny, who is the new object of his affections. Though Henry doubtless appreciates Fanny's fine qualities more with every passing day, he is more caught up in the thrill of the hunt: Fanny is his prey, and Henry is using every known technique to ensnare her. It would be chilling if Jane Austen didn't allow us to see that Fanny's heart is protected by her first love, Edmund.

Henry's plot to ensnare Fanny bears similarities to the Pharisees' many attempts to trap Jesus. In Matthew 12, they coyly suggest that Jesus' ability to cast out demons is possibly of sinful origin. Jesus responds in righteous anger: "You brood of vipers! How can you speak good, when you are evil?" (v. 34). By identifying them as *vipers*, Jesus is equating them with snakes who lure their prey in gradually, then inject poison and watch them die an agonizing death.

Vipers like Henry Crawford and the Pharisees are masters at poisoning others with the venom of hypocrisy and blasphemy. As believers, we must protect ourselves from this by safeguarding our hearts—and there is no better way to do this than by staying true to our first love, Jesus. This means abiding with Him, setting our moral compass by Scripture, and following Jesus' example in word, deed, and thought.

If you struggle with discerning truth from deception, ask the Holy Spirit for His help. He will teach you to recognize vipers and keep your heart safe from contamination.

❧

"WHEN THE SPIRIT OF TRUTH COMES, HE WILL GUIDE
YOU INTO ALL THE TRUTH . . . AND HE WILL DECLARE
TO YOU THE THINGS THAT ARE TO COME."

John 16:13

Emma made as slight a reply as she could; but it was fully sufficient for Mrs. Elton, who only wanted to be talking herself.

"So extremely like Maple Grove! And it is not merely the house—the grounds, I assure you, as far as I could observe, are strikingly like. The laurels at Maple Grove are in the same profusion as here, and stand very much in the same way—just across the lawn; and I had a glimpse of a fine large tree, with a bench round it, which put me so exactly in mind! My brother and sister will be enchanted with this place. People who have extensive grounds themselves are always pleased with any thing in the same style."

Emma doubted the truth of this sentiment. She had a great idea that people who had extensive grounds themselves cared very little for the extensive grounds of any body else; but it was not worth while to attack an error so double-dyed, and therefore only said in reply,

"When you have seen more of this country, I am afraid you will think you have overrated Hartfield. Surry is full of beauties."

"Oh! yes, I am quite aware of that. It is the garden of England, you know. Surry is the garden of England."

"Yes; but we must not rest our claims on that distinction. Many counties, I believe, are called the garden of England, as well as Surry."

"No, I fancy not," replied Mrs. Elton, with a most satisfied smile. "I never heard any county but Surry called so."

Emma was silenced.

—Emma

In Mrs. Elton, it seems that Emma has met her nemesis. The irony is that beneath the surface, the two have a great many similarities. Both place high value on social status, both care about outward appearances, and both are quick to rush to judgment. But in one very important way, Emma is far superior to Mrs. Elton: she has manners.

This distinction derives in part from Emma's higher social class—Mrs. Elton brags about her rich relatives and acquaintances to compensate for her own lack. But it also hearkens back to a certain sensitivity in Emma: her character is subtly being shaped by well-mannered friends like Mr. Knightley. Mrs. Elton *fancies* herself well-mannered; but next to Emma, her mannerisms are a cheap imitation.

As believers, you and I are both born into royalty—we are *daughters* of the King—and enjoy the privilege of walking with Jesus daily. When we allow Him to shape our character and mold our thoughts and actions, we develop the mannerisms of godly womanhood.

Listen to how the author of Proverbs describes a godly woman:

> Strength and honor are her clothing;
> She shall rejoice in time to come.
> She opens her mouth with wisdom,
> And on her tongue is the law of kindness.
> (31:25–26 NKJV)

We don't become women of strength, honor, and wisdom overnight; it requires self-discipline and godly surrender. But a godly heritage is yours; don't settle for cheap imitations.

❧

LET YOUR GENTLENESS BE KNOWN TO ALL MEN.

Philippians 4:5 NKJV

Taming Your Temper

"I cannot give you credit for any philosophy of the kind. Your retrospections must be so totally void of reproach, that the contentment arising from them is not of philosophy, but, what is much better, of innocence. But with me, it is not so. Painful recollections will intrude which cannot, which ought not, to be repelled. I have been a selfish being all my life, in practice, though not in principle. As a child I was taught what was right, but I was not taught to correct my temper. I was given good principles, but left to follow them in pride and conceit. Unfortunately an only son (for many years an only child), I was spoilt by my parents, who, though good themselves (my father, particularly, all that was benevolent and amiable), allowed, encouraged, almost taught me to be selfish and overbearing; to care for none beyond my own family circle; to think meanly of all the rest of the world; to wish at least to think meanly of their sense and worth compared with my own. Such I was, from eight to eight and twenty; and such I might still have been but for you, dearest, loveliest Elizabeth! What do I not owe you! You taught me a lesson, hard indeed at first, but most advantageous. By you, I was properly humbled. I came to you without a doubt of my reception. You shewed me how insufficient were all my pretensions to please a woman worthy of being pleased."

—*Pride and Prejudice*

The humility Darcy demonstrates in this repartee with Elizabeth is all we need to love him completely. Darcy admits to having grown up selfish: raised with good principles but allowed to follow them pridefully; spoiled by his parents; allowed to view outsiders with arrogance and disdain. But perhaps most significant is Darcy's admission that his temper was never corrected as a child. This lack of self-discipline in childhood, combined with cultivated prideful behavior, explains the conceit we see in him at the beginning of *Pride and Prejudice*. Fortunately for our hero, he met his match in feisty Lizzy and is now "properly humbled." Or at least, he is on his way.

The book of Proverbs is filled with warnings about letting our tempers get away. Perhaps one of the simplest and most straightforward is found in chapter 14: "A quick-tempered man does foolish things" (v. 17 NIV). Darcy's initial foolishness was manifested in a hurtful observation about Elizabeth; and when he first proposed, he was quick to voice criticism of her family. As with many of us, Darcy's battle to tame his tongue will be long and uphill.

For Christians, there are several important reasons to learn control over our tempers, but the most important is that we are to be imitators of Christ. This cannot be accomplished without spiritual maturity, which first requires a deep understanding and persistent application of Scriptures.

Do you struggle with a temper that sometimes leaps out of control? Are you quick to take offense or to criticize? Steep yourself in the Word, ask God for guidance, and choose not to let Satan have his way.

❧

Do not conform any longer to the pattern of this world, but be transformed by the renewing of your mind. Then you will be able to test and approve what God's will is—his good, pleasing and perfect will.

Romans 12:2 NIV

FREE TO LIVE IN FREEDOM

[Mary Crawford:] "I do not suppose I have worn [this necklace] six times: it is very pretty, but I never think of it; and though you would be most heartily welcome to any other in my trinket-box, you have happened to fix on the very one which, if I have a choice, I would rather part with and see in your possession than any other. Say no more against it, I entreat you. Such a trifle is not worth half so many words."

Fanny dared not make any farther opposition; and with renewed but less happy thanks accepted the necklace again, for there was an expression in Miss Crawford's eyes which she could not be satisfied with.

It was impossible for her to be insensible of Mr. Crawford's change of manners. She had long seen it. He evidently tried to please her: he was gallant, he was attentive, he was something like what he had been to her cousins: he wanted, she supposed, to cheat her of her tranquillity as he had cheated them; and whether he might not have some concern in this necklace—she could not be convinced that he had not, for Miss Crawford, complaisant as a sister, was careless as a woman and a friend.

Reflecting and doubting, and feeling that the possession of what she had so much wished for did not bring much satisfaction, she now walked home again, with a change rather than a diminution of cares since her treading that path before.

—Mansfield Park

anny is reluctantly accepting a gift from Mary Crawford—a delicate gold chain on which to wear a cross from her brother James. Why reluctantly? Because Fanny senses a motive behind the gift—a scheme created by Mary's brother, Henry (And she is right; time will reveal this.) But at the moment, Fanny has only her intuition to guide her . . . and it tells her that Henry's charm is a false front: "He was gallant [toward Fanny], he was attentive, he was something like what he had been to her cousins: he wanted, she supposed, to cheat her of her tranquillity as he had cheated them."

Had not Fanny observed closely while Henry flirted with Fanny's female cousins, she might not suspicion this truth. But she *saw* the havoc Henry wreaked: how he toyed with Maria's and Louisa's emotions, how they turned on one another in jealousy. And though Fanny may be flattered by Henry's charm (she *is* human, after all!), she cares more about the heart of the matter. Fanny understands that there is freedom in walking in the truth.

For believers, this is an intrinsic aspect of the greatest gift we'll ever receive: "It is for freedom that Christ has set us free" (Galatians 5:1 NIV). Do you see the promise in that statement? *For freedom, Jesus set us free!* Walking step-by-step with Christ and seeking His truth means recognizing His voice and enjoying the freedom found in Him. Because of His sacrifice, we can live free of bondage to our untrustworthy emotions, free of believing Satan's lies, free of any hindrances that keep us from becoming the women God wants us to be.

❧

"If you abide in my word, you are truly my disciples, and you will know the truth, and the truth will set you free. . . . So if the Son sets you free, you will be free indeed."

John 8:31–32, 36

Mrs. Ferrars was a little, thin woman, upright, even to formality, in her fig-ure, and serious, even to sourness, in her aspect. Her complexion was sallow; and her features small, without beauty, and naturally without expression; but a lucky contraction of the brow had rescued her countenance from the disgrace of insipidity, by giving it the strong characters of pride and ill nature. She was not a woman of many words; for, unlike people in general, she pro-portioned them to the number of her ideas; and of the few syllables that did escape her, not one fell to the share of Miss Dashwood, whom she eyed with the spirited determination of disliking her at all events.

Elinor could not now be made unhappy by this behaviour.—A few months ago it would have hurt her exceedingly; but it was not in Mrs. Ferrars' power to distress her by it now;—and the difference of her manners to the Miss Steeles, a difference which seemed purposely made to humble her more, only amused her. She could not but smile to see the graciousness of both mother and daughter towards the very person—for Lucy was particularly distin-guished—whom of all others, had they known as much as she did, they would have been most anxious to mortify; while she herself, who had comparatively no power to wound them, sat pointedly slighted by both.

—Sense and Sensibility

This chilling sketch of Mrs. Ferrars is enough to strike fear in the heart of any would-be daughter-in-law. One can just *see* her sallow complexion and small-featured face, her brow knitted with pride, her mean-spirited treatment of Elinor. To say nothing of her unconcealed favor-itism of Lucy Steele!

It is with great relief that we realize Elinor's heart is protected from the sting of Mrs. Ferrars's conduct. Months earlier, when her future hopes rested in one day becoming Mrs. Edward Ferrars, such treatment from his mother "would have hurt her exceedingly"; now, the scene unfolding before her causes only amusement. Such is the power of perspective when applied to time-chiseled character like Elinor's.

The Old Testament's Joseph also endured wrongful treatment and betrayal—a lifetime's worth! Sold into slavery by his brothers, baited endlessly by his employer's wife, and finally imprisoned wrongfully, Joseph had every right to wallow in bitterness and resentment.

But he chose to rise above his circumstances, to believe that God would make something good out of them. And God was with him through many years' toil, and eventually prospered his life as well as his character. Which is why, when Joseph came face-to-face with his brothers many years later, he was able to say, "You intended to harm me, but God intended it for good" (Genesis 50:20 NIV).

This can be as true in your life as it was for Joseph. If a certain person's actions are causing you grief or heartache, surrender that situation to the Father. Choose to pray for that person, and to praise God even in your difficult circumstances. Remember, what man intends for evil, God can use for good—the key lies in entrusting Him with the outcome.

❧

FINALLY, ALL OF YOU, LIVE IN HARMONY WITH ONE
ANOTHER; BE SYMPATHETIC, LOVE AS BROTHERS,
BE COMPASSIONATE AND HUMBLE. DO NOT REPAY
EVIL WITH EVIL OR INSULT WITH INSULT, BUT WITH
BLESSING, BECAUSE TO THIS YOU WERE CALLED SO
THAT YOU MAY INHERIT A BLESSING.

1 Peter 3:8–9 NIV

THE ART OF GOOD TIMING

Elizabeth could not help smiling at his easy manner of directing his friend.

"Did you speak from your own observation," said she, "when you told him that my sister loved him, or merely from my information last spring?"

"From the former. I had narrowly observed her during the two visits which I had lately made here; and I was convinced of her affection."

"And your assurance of it, I suppose, carried immediate conviction to him."

"It did. Bingley is most unaffectedly modest. His diffidence had prevented his depending on his own judgment in so anxious a case, but his reliance on mine made every thing easy. I was obliged to confess one thing, which for a time, and not unjustly, offended him. I could not allow myself to conceal that your sister had been in town three months last winter, that I had known it, and purposely kept it from him. He was angry. But his anger, I am persuaded, lasted no longer than he remained in any doubt of your sister's sentiments. He has heartily forgiven me now."

Elizabeth longed to observe that Mr. Bingley had been a most delightful friend; so easily guided that his worth was invaluable; but she checked herself. She remembered that he had yet to learn to be laughed at, and it was rather too early to begin. In anticipating the happiness of Bingley, which of course was to be inferior only to his own, he continued the conversation till they reached the house. In the hall they parted.

—*Pride and Prejudice*

mid this warm discussion over Bingley and Jane's recent engagement, we see Elizabeth hold back in teasing her future husband: "She checked herself. She remembered that he had yet to learn to be laughed at, and it was rather too early to begin." Already, it seems, Lizzy has learned when to hold her tongue and how to use timing to her advantage. Her choice bodes well for her future as Darcy's wife and lady of Pemberley.

In Christian circles, the ideal wife is often described as a Proverbs 31 woman. As pertains to a godly marriage, a key element of this woman's character is found in verses 11–12: "The heart of her husband trusts in her, and he will have no lack of gain She does him good, and not harm, all the days of her life."

Like Elizabeth, the Proverbs 31 wife knows how to be playful and loving with her husband, but she has good timing. What she doesn't do is provoke, taunt, or mock him, either face-to-face or to her friends. Being a woman who fears God above all things, she realizes that "doing him good" is an honor—that she bears the singular privilege of protecting his heart and gaining his trust as confidant, friend, and lover.

Do you think about how your words will affect your husband's spirit before you speak your mind, even in truth? Truly, it cannot be emphasized enough that a God-honoring marriage depends upon exercising good judgment, holding your tongue, and considering your husband's heart before responding impulsively.

❧

THE WISE WOMAN BUILDS HER HOUSE,
BUT WITH HER OWN HANDS THE FOOLISH ONE
TEARS HERS DOWN.

Proverbs 14:1 NIV

POOR JUDGE OF CHARACTER

"Do not you dance, Mr. Elton?" to which his prompt reply was, "Most readily, Mrs. Weston, if you will dance with me."

"Me!—oh! no—I would get you a better partner than myself. I am no dancer."

"If Mrs. Gilbert wishes to dance," said he, "I shall have great pleasure, I am sure—for, though beginning to feel myself rather an old married man, and that my dancing days are over, it would give me very great pleasure at any time to stand up with an old friend like Mrs. Gilbert."

"Mrs. Gilbert does not mean to dance, but there is a young lady disengaged whom I should be very glad to see dancing—Miss Smith."

"Miss Smith!—oh!—I had not observed.—You are extremely obliging—and if I were not an old married man.—But my dancing days are over, Mrs. Weston. You will excuse me. Any thing else I should be most happy to do, at your command—but my dancing days are over."

Mrs. Weston said no more; and Emma could imagine with what surprize and mortification she must be returning to her seat. This was Mr. Elton! the amiable, obliging, gentle Mr. Elton.—She looked round for a moment; he had joined Mr. Knightley at a little distance, and was arranging himself for settled conversation, while smiles of high glee passed between him and his wife.

She would not look again. Her heart was in a glow, and she feared her face might be as hot.

—Emma

Quite obviously, where Mr. Elton is concerned, Emma was a poor judge of character. To think that she once viewed him as "amiable, obliging, [and] gentle"! It is like a knife in her side to watch him openly scorn Harriet, and then to exchange "smiles of high glee" with his snooty wife.

Mr. Elton's behavior is shameful, but the circumstance could have been far worse: had the match between Harriet and Mr. Elton been successful, Emma would have been guilty of pairing Harriet with a man of deplorable character. Though they cannot see it now, Emma and Harriet are fortunate that the decision was made for them—and ostensibly, will learn a valuable lesson.

It is tempting not to see someone's true colors when we have reason not to. But one of the evidences of Christ's work in a believer's life is that He reveals the people He does not want in our lives. He opens ours eyes to things that we did not see before—malicious or gossiping behaviors, for example—and gives us a heart to despise those behaviors.

Spiritual maturity means preferring time with the Lord over negative influences that stunt our growth or cause us to stumble. As we walk in step with Him and seek to align our hearts with His, the result is that we seek fellowship with believers who also reflect godly qualities and strive to know Him more. The weightiness of this decision is seen in Proverbs 12:26, which says, "The righteous should choose his friends carefully, for the way of the wicked leads them astray" (NKJV).

☙

HE WHO WALKS WITH WISE MEN WILL BE WISE,
BUT THE COMPANION OF FOOLS WILL BE DESTROYED.

Proverbs 13:20 NKJV

AGAPE LOVE IN ACTION

[Edmund] would marry Miss Crawford. It was a stab, in spite of every long-standing expectation; and she was obliged to repeat again and again, that she was one of his two dearest, before the words gave her any sensation. Could [Fanny] believe Miss Crawford to deserve him, it would be—oh, how different would it be—how far more tolerable! But he was deceived in her: he gave her merits which she had not; her faults were what they had ever been, but he saw them no longer. Till she had shed many tears over this deception, Fanny could not subdue her agitation; and the dejection which followed could only be relieved by the influence of fervent prayers for his happiness.

It was her intention, as she felt it to be her duty, to try to overcome all that was excessive, all that bordered on selfishness, in her affection for Edmund. To call or to fancy it a loss, a disappointment, would be a presumption for which she had not words strong enough to satisfy her own humility. . . . She would endeavour to be rational, and to deserve the right of judging of Miss Crawford's character, and the privilege of true solicitude for him by a sound intellect and an honest heart.

—Mansfield Park

dmund has been deceived by Mary and is determined to marry her. This knowledge throws Fanny into agitation, tears, and dejection—but before much time has elapsed, she gathers herself enough to pray for her beloved Edmund. Her reaction demonstrates the truest form of love, flowing from an unselfish heart, with a pure motive and clear conscience.

Fanny's love for Edmund embodies the biblical notion of *agape* love: "Love is patient and kind; love does not envy or boast; it is not arrogant or rude. It does not insist on its own way; it is not irritable or resentful; it does not rejoice at wrongdoing, but rejoices with the truth. Love bears all things, believes all things, hopes all things, endures all things" (1 Corinthians 13:4–7). Agape love is *unselfish love*. It wishes the best for others even if it does not bring us happiness. It is a kind of love that allows Fanny to pray for Edmund, to hope that he will enjoy a loving, lasting marriage—even if it is not to her.

Agape love is love born of God, demonstrated to us in the person of Jesus, and abiding constantly in the Spirit. It is love in action. When we demonstrate it toward one another, we get to participate in demonstrating Christ to the world!

Agape love doesn't rely upon our emotions or circumstances for full expression. Rather, it is God's love—in essence, it reflects the very character and nature of God. Thus, the only way to show this kind of love ourselves is to look without wavering to the example of Jesus, who loved us first.

❧

BELOVED, LET US LOVE ONE ANOTHER, FOR LOVE IS
FROM GOD, AND WHOEVER LOVES HAS BEEN BORN OF
GOD AND KNOWS GOD. ANYONE WHO DOES NOT LOVE
DOES NOT KNOW GOD, BECAUSE GOD IS LOVE.

1 John 4:7–8

Behaving with Dignity

Elinor was prevented from making any reply to this civil triumph, by the door's being thrown open, the servant's announcing Mr. Ferrars, and Edward's immediately walking in.

It was a very awkward moment; and the countenance of each shewed that it was so. They all looked exceedingly foolish; and Edward seemed to have as great an inclination to walk out of the room again, as to advance farther into it. The very circumstance, in its unpleasantest form, which they would each have been most anxious to avoid, had fallen on them.—They were not only all three together, but were together without the relief of any other person. The ladies recovered themselves first. It was not Lucy's business to put herself forward, and the appearance of secrecy must still be kept up. She could therefore only look her tenderness, and after slightly addressing him, said no more.

But Elinor had more to do; and so anxious was she, for his sake and her own, to do it well, that she forced herself, after a moment's recollection, to welcome him, with a look and manner that were almost easy, and almost open; and another struggle, another effort still improved them. She would not allow the presence of Lucy, nor the consciousness of some injustice towards herself, to deter her from saying that she was happy to see him, and that she had very much regretted being from home, when he called before in Berkeley Street. She would not be frightened from paying him those attentions which, as a friend and almost a relation, were his due.

—*Sense and Sensibility*

Three young people, all pawns in a love triangle, sit awkwardly together for the first time: Edward, Elinor, and Lucy Steele. Lucy and Edward are secretly engaged; Edward and Elinor are secretly in love. All are bound by social customs to remain silent.

Poor Elinor trembles here with good reason: she loves Edward, and is aware that Lucy has somehow trapped him in a foolish engagement. Furthermore, she knows that Edward is too much a gentleman to break off an engagement—even a childhood engagement thoughtlessly made to a coarse, unrefined girl like Lucy Steele.

Elinor's hope of becoming Edward's wife feels lost forever, but she is also Edward's friend. Though Lucy watches through narrowed eyes, Elinor greets Edward warmly, with the grace and dignity that is engrained in her character.

The behavior of the Proverbs 31 woman aligns closely with Elinor's conduct: "She is clothed with strength and dignity; she can *laugh at the days to come*" (v. 25 NIV, emphasis added). A woman who trusts the Lord for the outcome can laugh freely because she knows that the future is in His hands. No matter what happens, God can be trusted.

Can you say without hesitation that you trust God enough to laugh at whatever *your* future holds? Does your eternal hope rest in Him, or are you fixated on getting what you want in the moment? Becoming a godly woman means *choosing* the joy of the Lord over self-pity, timidity, or fear. Not because life is perfect, but because our happiness is not measured by our circumstances. It is anchored in Him.

❧

SHE SPEAKS WITH WISDOM,
AND FAITHFUL INSTRUCTION IS ON HER TONGUE.

Proverbs 31:26 NIV

Pursuing Perfection

[Anne] never could accept him. And it was not only that her feelings were still adverse to any man save one; her judgement, on a serious consideration of the possibilities of such a case was against Mr. Elliot.

Though they had now been acquainted a month, she could not be satisfied that she really knew his character. That he was a sensible man, an agreeable man, that he talked well, professed good opinions, seemed to judge properly and as a man of principle, this was all clear enough. He certainly knew what was right, nor could she fix on any one article of moral duty evidently transgressed; but yet she would have been afraid to answer for his conduct. She distrusted the past, if not the present. The names which occasionally dropt of former associates, the allusions to former practices and pursuits, suggested suspicions not favourable of what he had been. She saw that there had been bad habits; that Sunday travelling had been a common thing; that there had been a period of his life (and probably not a short one) when he had been, at least, careless in all serious matters; and, though he might now think very differently, who could answer for the true sentiments of a clever, cautious man, grown old enough to appreciate a fair character? How could it ever be ascertained that his mind was truly cleansed?

Mr. Elliot was rational, discreet, polished, but he was not open. There was never any burst of feeling, any warmth of indignation or delight, at the evil or good of others. This, to Anne, was a decided imperfection. Her early impressions were incurable. She prized the frank, the open-hearted, the eager character beyond all others. Warmth and enthusiasm did captivate her still. She felt that she could so much more depend upon the sincerity of those who sometimes looked or said a careless or a hasty thing, than of those whose presence of mind never varied, whose tongue never slipped.

—*Persuasion*

Though Anne was cautiously approving of Mr. Elliot when they first met, time spent together has revealed him to be a cold, calculated, emotionless man. "*Too perfect*," we might say—too ready with the right response or excuse or rationalization. Among the flaws Anne observes are glimpses of former bad habits, like "Sunday traveling" (missing church) and a carelessness "in all serious matters." He is not the perfect creature he appears to be, but he certainly works hard to create that illusion. Only time will reveal Mr. Elliot's true character.

The desire to "look perfect" is a driving force for many of us. While we might laugh off the suggestion that we could ever come close to achieving perfection, aspiring to be *perceived* as perfect is the secret motivation behind many of our choices. After all, we want to be successful at what we do, whether it's as an employee, or raising children, or running a household, or volunteering, or helping at church.

On the surface, there is nothing wrong with this goal. But when we grow frantic trying to get everything done *and* make it look easy, we sacrifice more than our own sanity: we miss out on seeing God glorified in our weakness. Paul understood this concept and embraced it as his life philosophy: "But he said to me, 'My grace is sufficient for you, for my power is made perfect in weakness'" (2 Corinthians 12:9).

An unwillingness to allow yourself to fail at anything, or to let anyone else *see* that you have failed, is a key indicator that your heart does not trust God with the outcome. Admitting weakness can be difficult, but allowing God glory through your weakness is a reward beyond compare.

❦

THEREFORE I WILL BOAST ALL THE MORE GLADLY OF MY
WEAKNESSES, SO THAT THE POWER OF CHRIST MAY REST UPON ME.

2 Corinthians 12:9

TEMPERING THE HEART

In a few minutes [Darcy] approached the table where [Lizzy] was sitting with Kitty; and, while pretending to admire her work said in a whisper, "Go to your father, he wants you in the library." She was gone directly.

Her father was walking about the room, looking grave and anxious. "Lizzy," said he, "what are you doing? Are you out of your senses, to be accepting this man? Have not you always hated him?"

How earnestly did she then wish that her former opinions had been more reasonable, her expressions more moderate! It would have spared her from explanations and professions which it was exceedingly awkward to give; but they were now necessary, and she assured him, with some confusion, of her attachment to Mr. Darcy.

"Or, in other words, you are determined to have him. He is rich, to be sure, and you may have more fine clothes and fine carriages than Jane. But will they make you happy?"

"Have you any other objection," said Elizabeth, "than your belief of my indifference?"

"None at all. We all know him to be a proud, unpleasant sort of man; but this would be nothing if you really liked him."

"I do, I do like him," she replied, with tears in her eyes, "I love him. Indeed he has no improper pride. He is perfectly amiable. You do not know what he really is; then pray do not pain me by speaking of him in such terms."

—Pride and Prejudice

r. Darcy has requested Lizzy's hand from her father, and now Mr. Bennet wants to hear from his daughter. Understandably, he is perplexed by this turn of events: "Are you out of your senses, to be accepting this man? Have not you always hated him?" Through standing tears, Lizzy conveys her regret in having spoken impulsively, angrily, and without moderation toward Darcy. She reiterates her love for Darcy and can rejoice in having learned the valuable lesson of a softened heart.

To understand the concept of having a soft heart, we should first look at the alternative. A "hard" heart conjures words like *rebellion, arrogance,* and *inflexibility*—all appropriately used to describe both Elizabeth and Darcy in various points throughout the novel.

The numerous advantages to having a soft heart are seen in the parable of the sower in Matthew 13: "A farmer planted seed. As he scattered the seed, some of it fell on the road, and birds ate it. Some fell in the gravel; it sprouted quickly but didn't put down roots, so when the sun came up it withered just as quickly. Some fell in the weeds; as it came up, it was strangled by the weeds. Some fell on good earth, and produced a harvest beyond his wildest dreams" (vv. 3–8 MSG).

A soft heart is like rich soil that produces bountiful yield, while a cold heart repels the good things brought to it. The key to keeping the right heart is found in total submission to God—trusting in His will, His way, and His means.

Strive to maintain a teachable heart. Let the lessons in your life shape you rather than harden you. Only a soft heart has the capacity to fully give and receive God's love, peace, and joy.

৽৽

BUT HE KNOWS THE WAY THAT I TAKE;
WHEN HE HAS TRIED ME, I SHALL COME OUT AS GOLD.

Job 23:10

SOJOURNERS ON EARTH

When [Fanny] had been coming to Portsmouth, she had loved to call it her home, had been fond of saying that she was going home; the word had been very dear to her, and so it still was, but it must be applied to Mansfield. That was now the home. Portsmouth was Portsmouth; Mansfield was home.

They had been long so arranged in the indulgence of her secret meditations, and nothing was more consolatory to her than to find her aunt using the same language: "I cannot but say I much regret your being from home at this distressing time, so very trying to my spirits. I trust and hope, and sincerely wish you may never be absent from home so long again," were most delightful sentences to her. Still, however, it was her private regale. Delicacy to her parents made her careful not to betray such a preference of her uncle's house. It was always: "When I go back into Northamptonshire, or when I return to Mansfield, I shall do so and so." For a great while it was so, but at last the longing grew stronger, it overthrew caution, and she found herself talking of what she should do when she went home before she was aware. She reproached herself, coloured, and looked fearfully towards her father and mother. She need not have been uneasy. There was no sign of displeasure, or even of hearing her. They were perfectly free from any jealousy of Mansfield. She was as welcome to wish herself there as to be there.

—*Mansfield Park*

During her eight years at Mansfield Park, Fanny always felt like a visitor. But a three-month-long visit to her childhood home in Portsmouth has allowed her the delicious realization that Mansfield Park is truly "home." No longer a wanderer, Fanny is free to embrace Mansfield as her next and final destination (a prescient allusion to her future with Edmund!).

As believers, we are also in search of a final destination—but it will not be found on Earth, nor in this lifetime. We understand the heart of the psalmist's declaration, "I am a sojourner on the earth" (Psalm 119:19); we simply aren't home yet. We are travelers, doing battle every day with failing bodies, corrupt political systems, poverty, squalor, chaos—all the deficiencies of living in a fallen world.

Do you ever feel an unexplainable homesickness? God designed us not to feel at peace in this world, but to always harbor homesickness. Our final resting place, heaven, will be the full manifestation of perfection. We will finally enjoy all that is missing here.

Though it's easy to get comfortable when our lives are going well, we should invite that longing, that tug on our hearts, that ache in our throats: it is the living hope that something better awaits us. Remember, we're foreigners here. An existence not marred by imperfection or inadequacy is coming. A place that will know no more tears, no more sorrow. An eternity of communing freely with the God of the universe!

⟡

HE WILL WIPE AWAY EVERY TEAR FROM THEIR EYES,
AND DEATH SHALL BE NO MORE, NEITHER SHALL THERE
BE MOURNING, NOR CRYING, NOR PAIN ANYMORE, FOR
THE FORMER THINGS HAVE PASSED AWAY.

Revelation 21:4

A SPOILED LEGACY

The following day brought news from Richmond to throw every thing else into the background. An express arrived at Randalls to announce the death of Mrs. Churchill! Though her nephew had had no particular reason to hasten back on her account, she had not lived above six-and-thirty hours after his return. A sudden seizure of a different nature from any thing foreboded by her general state, had carried her off after a short struggle. The great Mrs. Churchill was no more.

It was felt as such things must be felt. Every body had a degree of gravity and sorrow; tenderness towards the departed, solicitude for the surviving friends; and, in a reasonable time, curiosity to know where she would be buried. Goldsmith tells us, that when a lovely woman stoops to folly, she has nothing to do but to die; and when she stoops to be disagreeable, it is equally to be recommended as a clearer of ill-fame. Mrs. Churchill, after being disliked at least twenty-five years, was now spoken of with compassionate allowances. In one point she was fully justified. She had never been admitted before to be seriously ill. The event acquitted her of all the fancifulness, and all the selfishness of imaginary complaints.

"Poor Mrs. Churchill!"

—Emma

Though we never actually meet or hear Mrs. Churchill speak in *Emma*, we know enough about her to dislike her: she is a demanding, unreasonable matriarch whose ill temper and iron-fisted rule led to a spoiled legacy. Only in death is her character offered a reprieve: "Mrs.

Churchill, after being disliked at least twenty-five years, was now spoken of with compassionate allowances."

In Mrs. Churchill's life, we see how indulging in pride and temper can destroy one's character; but even more, we see how it can negatively affect our legacy.

In 2 Chronicles 33–34, we see an interesting progression within three generations of kings. First, Manasseh brought in idols from foreign lands but repented to the Lord at the end of his life. Then, his son Amon ruled with a hard heart and eventually his own men attacked and killed him. Finally, Josiah—who watched his father and grandfather carefully—determined to lead better as a king and a follower of God. In the thirty-one years Josiah ruled, he returned Jerusalem to its rightful place, cleared the temple of false gods, and led the Israelites in worship back to the heart of God. Josiah built a solid legacy based on personal, faithful commitment to the one true God.

As Christ followers, we have a responsibility to exemplify Christ to those around us. The faithfulness that we display in our walk with God could ostensibly lead others to Christ—or it could deter them from seeking a relationship with Him. Think of the eternal ramifications of that! Which legacy will you leave?

⁌⁘⁙

[JOSIAH] STOOD BY HIS PILLAR AND RENEWED THE
COVENANT IN THE PRESENCE OF THE LORD—TO
FOLLOW THE LORD AND KEEP HIS COMMANDS,
REGULATIONS AND DECREES WITH ALL HIS HEART
AND ALL HIS SOUL, AND TO OBEY THE WORDS OF THE
COVENANT WRITTEN IN THIS BOOK.

2 Chronicles 34:31 NIV

SEEKING REPENTANCE

*"My illness has made me think. . . . I considered the past: I saw in my own
behaviour, since the beginning of our acquaintance with him last autumn,
nothing but a series of imprudence towards myself, and want of kindness to
others. I saw that my own feelings had prepared my sufferings, and that my
want of fortitude under them had almost led me to the grave. . . .*

*"I wonder at my recovery,—wonder that the very eagerness of my desire
to live, to have time for atonement to my God, and to you all, did not kill
me at once. Had I died,—in what peculiar misery should I have left you, my
nurse, my friend, my sister!—You, who had seen all the fretful selfishness
of my latter days; who had known all the murmurings of my heart!—How
should I have lived in your remembrance!—My mother too! How could you
have consoled her!—I cannot express my own abhorrence of myself.*

*"Whenever I looked towards the past, I saw some duty neglected, or
some failing indulged. Every body seemed injured by me. The kindness, the
unceasing kindness of Mrs. Jennings, I had repaid with ungrateful contempt.
To the Middletons, to the Palmers, the Steeles, to every common acquaintance even, I had been insolent and unjust; with a heart hardened against
their merits, and a temper irritated by their very attention.—To John, to
Fanny,—yes, even to them, little as they deserve, I had given less than their
due. But you,—you above all, above my mother, had been wronged by me."*

—*Sense and Sensibility*

The moment of repentance is upon Marianne—and
what a bitter pill it is. During her long illness and recovery, her eyes were opened to her foolhardy choices: her
actions, her imprudences, even the thoughts that she allowed

free rein where she should have shown restraint. Now she is torn apart by the realization of all whom she hurt with her behavior. "Every body seemed injured by me," she tells Elinor.

Marianne herself labels her own behavior "fretful self-ishness" and agonizes to think that she almost killed herself in her single-minded pursuit of Willoughby. She marvels that she was spared from death by a merciful God before she had a chance to make atonement, and she shudders at how deeply her selfishness hurt her beloved Elinor.

Each of us has, in some way and at some time, been in Marianne's shoes—a position where our selfish behavior wrought painful consequences. By now Marianne has acknowledged her part and shown remorse, yet still she agonizes—and rightly so.

As with Marianne, it sometimes takes deep hurt to teach us important lessons about repentance. After all, if it weren't for the pain of the mistake, would we truly appreciate God's overwhelming gift of forgiveness? In the biblical story about Zacchaeus, a stingy tax collector who took advantage of his fellow men, we're reminded that the gift of forgiveness is a free gift offered to *all* sinners: "For the Son of Man came to seek and to save what was lost" (Luke 19:10 NIV). This simple statement should cause us to rejoice because offenses great and small mean one thing in God's eyes: sin. And it is sin that we're set free from, through His sacrifice.

Take a moment to let this sink in: the gift of forgiveness was paid for by Christ on the cross. Think about what this sacrifice really means to you—what you are saved from, and what you are saved *to*. Then rejoice!

❧

"Today salvation has come to this house, because this man, too, is a son of Abraham."

Luke 19:9 NIV

Making Light of Sin

[Edmund:] "[Mary] reprobated her brother's folly in being drawn on by a woman whom he had never cared for, to do what must lose him the woman he adored; but still more the folly of poor Maria, in sacrificing such a situation, plunging into such difficulties, under the idea of being really loved by a man who had long ago made his indifference clear. Guess what I must have felt. To hear the woman whom—no harsher name than folly given! So voluntarily, so freely, so coolly to canvass it! No reluctance, no horror, no feminine, shall I say, no modest loathings? This is what the world does. For where, Fanny, shall we find a woman whom nature had so richly endowed? Spoilt, spoilt!"

After a little reflection, he went on with a sort of desperate calmness. "I will tell you everything, and then have done for ever. She saw it only as folly, and that folly stamped only by exposure. The want of common discretion, of caution: his going down to Richmond for the whole time of her being at Twickenham; her putting herself in the power of a servant; it was the detection, in short—oh, Fanny! it was the detection, not the offence, which she reprobated. It was the imprudence which had brought things to extremity, and obliged her brother to give up every dearer plan in order to fly with her."

—Mansfield Park

In Mary's cool reaction to a disgraceful choice (her brother Henry has run away with the married Maria Rushworth), Edmund finally sees Mary for who she is. For too long he was blind to her character flaws, but hearing Mary lightly label the lovers' sin as simply "folly" finally opens this preacher's eyes to the truth.

Mary Crawford's view on sin reflects moral relativism, which is quick to quote Jesus' words "Judge not, that you be not judged" (Matthew 7:1) but ignore His warning that "unless you repent, you will all likewise perish" (Luke 13:3). In other words, it is the inclination to treat sin lightly and neither repent nor seek forgiveness.

Jesus loves us enough to chasten us. Clergyman Edmund knows this, though he recognizes nearly too late that the woman he "loves" (for it is a deceived kind of love) does not. Luckily, Edmund sees the impossibility of a future with this woman and sees that relativism has spoiled her character: "No reluctance, no horror, no feminine, shall I say, no modest loathings? This is what the world does."

As believers, we need to be on our guard against allowing this hardening—"what the world does"—to happen to us too. If we do not, we will gradually become like the lukewarm Christians in Laodicea, whom Jesus blisteringly reproached: "So, because you are lukewarm, and neither hot nor cold, I will spit you out of my mouth" (Revelation 3:16). Better to be horrified by sin and steer brothers and sisters toward repentance than justify it and be spit out of God's mouth!

❦

"AS MANY AS I LOVE, I REBUKE AND CHASTEN.
THEREFORE BE ZEALOUS AND REPENT."

Revelation 3:19 NKJV

IRON SHARPENS IRON

While waiting for the carriage, she found Mr. Knightley by her side. He looked around, as if to see that no one were near, and then said, "Emma . . . how could you be so unfeeling to Miss Bates? How could you be so insolent in your wit to a woman of her character, age, and situation?—Emma, I had not thought it possible."

Emma recollected, blushed, was sorry, but tried to laugh it off. "Nay, how could I help saying what I did?—Nobody could have helped it. It was not so very bad. I dare say she did not understand me."

"I assure you she did. . . . Were she your equal in situation—but, Emma, consider how far this is from being the case. She is poor; she has sunk from the comforts she was born to; and, if she lived to old age, must probably sink more. Her situation should secure your compassion. It was badly done, indeed! You, whom she had known from an infant, whom she had seen grow up from a period when her notice was an honour, to have you now, in thoughtless spirits, and the pride of the moment, laugh at her, humble her—and before her niece, too—and before others, many of whom (certainly some,) would be entirely guided by your treatment of her.—This is not pleasant to you, Emma—and it is very far from pleasant to me; but I must, I will,—I will tell you truths while I can; satisfied with proving myself your friend by very faithful counsel, and trusting that you will some time or other do me greater justice than you can do now."

—Emma

Fresh air, camaraderie, and a delightful repast—all combine to offers a glimpse at celebrating out-of-doors in the nineteenth century, when picnicking was beginning to gain fashion. But the merriment takes a dark turn when, following the telling sentence "Emma could not resist," our heroine indulges in a biting retort intended to humiliate the talkative Miss Bates.

This brings about Mr. Knightley's tongue-lashing: "It was badly done, indeed!" At no other point in the book does he speak so harshly to Emma—an indication that he is troubled by what he sees emerging in her character.

To Emma's credit, this scene represents a turning point. Her heart, while pierced by Mr. Knightley's sharp words, is prepared to receive his reproof. It is testament to her deep respect for the gentleman that his rebuke shakes her. Their relationship is a reflection of Proverbs 27:6: "Faithful are the wounds of a friend; profuse are the kisses of an enemy." In light of the shallow relationships she has nurtured with Harriet and Frank, Emma realizes that Mr. Knightley's approval of her integrity matters more than false flattery.

How important it is to choose friends who choose to speak honestly in love, rather than fill us with shallow falsehoods. When we seek wise counsel and cultivate Christ-centered friendships, we can say (and mean): "Let a righteous man strike me—it is a kindness; let him rebuke me—it is oil for my head; let my head not refuse it" (Psalm 141:5). Do the friends in your life bear this privilege?

❦

As iron sharpens iron,
so a man sharpens the countenance of his friend.

Proverbs 27:17 NKJV

BEAUTY OF A TEACHABLE SPIRIT

[Catherine:] "Your sister taught me; I cannot tell how. Mrs. Allen used to take pains, year after year, to make me like them; but I never could, till I saw them the other day in Milsom Street; I am naturally indifferent about flowers."

[Henry:] "But now you love a hyacinth. So much the better. You have gained a new source of enjoyment, and it is well to have as many holds upon happiness as possible. Besides, a taste for flowers is always desirable in your sex, as a means of getting you out of doors, and tempting you to more frequent exercise than you would otherwise take. And though the love of a hyacinth may be rather domestic, who can tell, the sentiment once raised, but you may in time come to love a rose?"

"But I do not want any such pursuit to get me out of doors. The pleasure of walking and breathing fresh air is enough for me, and in fine weather I am out more than half my time. Mamma says I am never within."

"At any rate, however, I am pleased that you have learnt to love a hyacinth. The mere habit of learning to love is the thing; and a teachableness of disposition in a young lady is a great blessing."

—Northanger Abbey

This conversation between Catherine and Henry is about more than Catherine's "learning to love a hyacinth"—a flower to which she was naturally indifferent before meeting the Tilneys and coming to visit Northanger Abbey. The greater context here is that Catherine has received an education; she has improved her intellect, reasoning, and taste. This transformation is best summarized by Henry's statement, "The mere habit of learning to love is the thing; and a teachableness of disposition in a young lady is a great blessing."

Catherine came to Northanger Abbey a simple country girl with high ideals and an impressionable spirit. Under Henry's tutelage, she has matured beyond fantasizing about horror novels into a woman who responds graciously and gracefully to teaching moments.

Like Catherine, we are best poised to grow and mature in godly wisdom when we demonstrate a teachable spirit before the Lord. In Psalm 86:11, David wrote, "Teach me Your way, O Lord; I will walk in Your truth; unite my heart to fear Your name" (NKJV). In this verse David is essentially saying, *I can't know Your way, Lord, unless You show me.* Within this posture he is demonstrating appropriate awe before God's greatness, as well as an awareness of his own sinfulness. It is a perfect example of recognizing that the only way to live holy, upright lives is to let God go before us and to follow Him intimately.

Do you desire a teachable spirit? You will find that the more time you spend in prayer and Scripture, the less you actually "know"—and the greater your sweet dependence on Christ will become.

⁂

THE FEAR OF THE LORD IS THE BEGINNING OF WISDOM,
AND THE KNOWLEDGE OF THE HOLY ONE IS UNDERSTANDING.

Proverbs 9:10 NKJV

GODLY MENTORING

Kitty, to her very material advantage, spent the chief of her time with her two elder sisters. In society so superior to what she had generally known, her improvement was great. She was not of so ungovernable a temper as Lydia [now Mrs. Wickham]; and, removed from the influence of Lydia's example, she became, by proper attention and management, less irritable, less ignorant, and less insipid. From the farther disadvantage of Lydia's society she was of course carefully kept, and though Mrs. Wickham frequently invited her to come and stay with her, with the promise of balls and young men, her father would never consent to her going.

Mary was the only daughter who remained at home; and she was necessarily drawn from the pursuit of accomplishments by Mrs. Bennet's being quite unable to sit alone. Mary was obliged to mix more with the world, but she could still moralize over every morning visit; and as she was no longer mortified by comparisons between her sisters' beauty and her own, it was suspected by her father that she submitted to the change without much reluctance.

As for Wickham and Lydia, their characters suffered no revolution from the marriage of her sisters. He bore with philosophy the conviction that Elizabeth must now become acquainted with whatever of his ingratitude and falsehood had before been unknown to her; and in spite of every thing, was not wholly without hope that Darcy might yet be prevailed on to make his fortune.

—Pride and Prejudice

In this conclusion to *Pride and Prejudice*, readers get a glimpse of the positive effects of Jane's and Elizabeth's healthy marriages upon the youngest two Bennet girls, Kitty and Mary. Through Kitty in particular do we see the benefits of being exposed to "society so superior to what she had generally known."

Is it any wonder Lydia ran away with Wickham? Bad influences *always* produce weak character. Certainly they cultivated in Kitty and Lydia an unquenchable self-importance, which culminated in Lydia's running away with Wickham.

Thankfully, it's never too late for positive influence, as we see in Jane and Elizabeth's tutelage of Kitty. Titus 2:3–5 illuminates the value of this arrangement: "Older women likewise are to be reverent in their behavior, not malicious gossips nor enslaved to much wine, teaching what is good, so that they may encourage the young women to love their husbands, to love their children, to be sensible, pure, workers at home, kind, being subject to their own husbands, so that the word of God will not be dishonored" (NASB).

A woman who is equipped to guide and shape the character of younger women will have a heart for the Lord and a burning desire to be in His Word and to follow Truth herself. Through Jane and Elizabeth, we see the improvements that this arrangement can bring to a young woman's character.

You have a responsibility, as a believer, to develop a godly reputation that is worth following. So pursue holiness to the glory of God, allow your heart to be dominated by Jesus' love, and imitate Him to become like Him. May your example be a bold proclamation of the gospel!

❧

ONE GENERATION SHALL COMMEND YOUR WORKS TO ANOTHER, AND SHALL DECLARE YOUR MIGHTY ACTS.

Psalm 145:4

PURSUING VANITY

"I do not know," said he, after a pause of expectation on [Elinor's] side, and thoughtfulness on his own,—"how you may have accounted for my behaviour to your sister, or what diabolical motive you may have imputed to me.— Perhaps you will hardly think the better of me,—it is worth the trial however, and you shall hear every thing. When I first became intimate in your family, I had no other intention, no other view in the acquaintance than to pass my time pleasantly while I was obliged to remain in Devonshire, more pleasantly than I had ever done before. Your sister's lovely person and interesting manners could not but please me; and her behaviour to me almost from the first, was of a kind—It is astonishing, when I reflect on what it was, and what she was, that my heart should have been so insensible! But at first I must confess, my vanity only was elevated by it. Careless of her happiness, thinking only of my own amusement, giving way to feelings which I had always been too much in the habit of indulging, I endeavoured, by every means in my power, to make myself pleasing to her, without any design of returning her affection."

—Sense and Sensibility

In this opening to a much longer scene—Willoughby's full confession to Elinor, while Marianne lies upstairs on her deathbed—we get our first real glimpse of a character whose motivation was heretofore unknown.

By Willoughby's own admission, his vanity controls his life. He has lived thinking only of his own amusements, indulging his feelings where convenient, and endeavoring to conquer whatever presents a challenge. And what has it brought him? Heartache, regret, and a loveless marriage.

In the book of Ecclesiastes, we are given an equally heartbreaking picture of a life guided by vanity. The once great King Solomon says, "Vanity of vanities, all is vanity" (1:2 NKJV). Solomon—not only a king, but a teacher of God's people—has sinned grievously in God's sight. The book of Ecclesiastes is his open admission of his folly, a warning to God's people to avoid the same face.

The reference to "vanity" refers not to God-given creature comforts, but rather the pursuit of happiness in *things* and *accomplishments*. The more wealth Solomon gained, the more disappointed he became; the more great acts he accomplished, the more fruitless it all felt. It is likely that with each conquest, Willoughby experienced the same hollow satisfaction. The guiding principle for both was a desire to please self, not God.

Unless fulfillment is sought from God, your soul will not find true happiness.

❦

NO MATTER HOW MUCH WE SEE, WE ARE NEVER
SATISFIED. NO MATTER HOW MUCH WE HEAR, WE
ARE NOT CONTENT . . . I OBSERVED EVERYTHING
GOING ON UNDER THE SUN, AND REALLY, IT IS ALL
MEANINGLESS—LIKE CHASING THE WIND.

Ecclesiastes 1:8, 14 NLT

An Honorable Legacy

Too late, [Sir Thomas] became aware how unfavourable to the character of any young people must be the totally opposite treatment which Maria and Julia had been always experiencing at home, where the excessive indulgence and flattery of their aunt had been continually contrasted with his own severity. . . .

Here had been grievous mismanagement; but, bad as it was, [Sir Thomas] gradually grew to feel that it had not been the most direful mistake in his plan of education. Something must have been wanting within, or time would have worn away much of its ill effect. He feared that principle, active principle, had been wanting; that they had never been properly taught to govern their inclinations and tempers by that sense of duty which can alone suffice. They had been instructed theoretically in their religion, but never required to bring it into daily practice. To be distinguished for elegance and accomplishments, the authorised object of their youth, could have had no useful influence that way, no moral effect on the mind. He had meant them to be good, but his cares had been directed to the understanding and manners, not the disposition; and of the necessity of self-denial and humility, he feared they had never heard from any lips that could profit them.

—Mansfield Park

As Sir Thomas looks over the ruinous choices of three of his four children, he is forced to recognize that his severe parenting was a misguided effort to offset the excessive indulgence of Aunt Norris. He also admits that—perhaps worst of all—his children were "instructed theoretically in their religion, but never required to bring it into daily practice."

King David's life offers a case study that every parent should examine. He too experienced an unprecedented number of successes in his professional and personal life, but he failed often as a husband and a parent. At the end of his life, David wrote, "Solomon, know the God of your father, and serve Him with a whole heart and a willing mind; for the LORD searches all hearts, and understands every intent of the thoughts. If you seek Him, He will let you find Him; but if you forsake Him, He will reject you forever" (1 Chronicles 28:9 NASB). David was essentially telling Solomon, "Learn from my mistakes. Make God your first love. *Nothing else matters.*"

There is hope in these two bleak examples, and the hope is this: each of us has the opportunity to correct the course and leave behind a strong spiritual legacy. That legacy is not about producing successful children or creating the perfect ministry or leading the most people to Christ. It is about loving God with *every facet of our lives.* Humbling ourselves enough to admit where we have fallen short and asking for forgiveness, and modeling Christlikeness everywhere: at home, at work, at church, at play. Making Christ first priority in every area of your life, so that whoever might be watching is inspired to do the same.

❧

BE CAREFUL TO DO ACCORDING TO ALL THAT IS
WRITTEN IN [THE BOOK OF LIFE]; FOR THEN
YOU WILL MAKE YOUR WAY PROSPEROUS, AND
THEN YOU WILL HAVE SUCCESS.

Joshua 1:8 NASB

J ANE AUSTEN was born in Steventon, Hampshire, England, December 1775, the seventh child (of eight) and second daughter (out of two) of the Reverend George and Cassandra Austen.

Eighteenth-century society, into which Austen was born, was a time when women were limited in their educational opportunities. Fortunately for Jane, she came from a household that valued education for both its sons and daughters. She was mostly schooled at home by her father and older brothers, and encouraged to produce literature and plays from an early age. Her early writing was often used as a form of entertainment for her older siblings.

The political climate of her lifespan saw great upheaval. Great Britain was embroiled in a growing conflict with the American colonies, spawning a struggle that would ultimately lead to the Revolutionary War—one of three wars involving Great Britain during Jane's lifetime. With two brothers serving in the Royal Navy and a third in the Militia, she understood the complex nature of war; yet surprisingly, the theme of war is rarely referenced in her novels.

In this way, and many others, Austen's personal life stood in contrast to her subject matter. She wrote of love and relationships, yet never married (she was engaged to longtime friend, Harris Bigg Wither, but she withdrew her offer the following day). While clever and pretty, she socialized very little; her biting literary remarks on human emotions, romance, and social obligations were drawn from the privacy of quiet home life.

For the daughter of an Anglican curate, Austen's novels contain very few direct references to religion or spirituality. However, her characters speak and act in ways that reflect the deeply rooted influences of church, morality, and God on nineteenth-century culture and on Jane herself. Upon close inspection, one glimpses frequent—if subtle—allusions to her Christian faith and church upbringing. Themes such as conviction, redemption, hypocrisy, and conscience further lend themselves beautifully to biblical observations and comparisons.

Jane became ill in early 1816 and was soon diagnosed with Addison's disease (however, her final illness has also been described as Hodgkin's lymphoma). On July 18, 1817, at only forty-one years of age, she died in her sister's arms. She was buried in Winchester Cathedral; the inscription on her grave reads as follows:

In memory of
JANE AUSTEN,
youngest daughter of the late
Revd. GEORGE AUSTEN,
formerly Rector of Steventon in this County.
She departed this Life on the 18th July 1817,
aged 41, after a long illness supported with
the patience and the hopes of a Christian.
The benevolence of her heart,
the sweetness of her temper, and
the extraordinary endowments of her mind
obtained the regard of all who knew her, and
the warmest love of her intimate connections.
Their grief is in proportion to their affection
they know their loss to be irreparable,
but in the deepest affliction they are consoled
by a firm though humble hope that her charity,
devotion, faith and purity have rendered
her soul acceptable in the sight of her
REDEEMER.

Timeline of Austen's novels:

Sense and Sensibility (1811)

Pride and Prejudice (1813)

Mansfield Park (1814)

Emma (1815)

Northanger Abbey and *Persuasion*
(1817, published posthumously)

✦

MAY WE NOW, AND ON EACH RETURN
OF NIGHT, CONSIDER HOW THE PAST
DAY HAS BEEN SPENT BY US, WHAT HAVE
BEEN OUR PREVAILING THOUGHTS,
WORDS, AND ACTIONS DURING IT.

—*Evening Prayer 1*